NO DEATH IN JESUS CHRIST

Jesus Christ is The Lord

Folake Hassan

The Righteous Publishing House

London UK

No Death In Jesus Christ

ISBN: 978-0-9928684-7-5

Published by The Righteous Publishing House

93 Villiers Road

Willesden. London NW2 5QB

APPRECIATION

I give all praises to God Almighty, who chose me and qualified me to be a Christian. I thank God for empowered me to study His Word and for blessing me with His Wisdom. My sincere appreciation also goes to the men and women from every part of the world that God has used to minister His Words to bless me. I thank my children and my late husband, Lanre Hassan for their support and good attitude that have enabled me to walk a good walk in my journey as a Christian. I thank my parents for taking good care of me through my childhood.

CONTENTS

INTRODUCTION 1

CHAPTER ONE....JESUS CHRIST IS THE LORD 5

CHAPTER TWO...PUTTING ON THE IMMORTALITY 23

CHAPTER THREE....THE WHOLE ARMOUR OF GOD 41

CHAPTER FOUR...THE POWER OF CONTINUITY 51

CHAPTER FIVE....FORGIVENESS IN CHRIST 67

CHAPTER SIX....THERE IS NO FEAR IN CHRIST 72

CHAPTER SEVEN...ARISE AND SHINE FOR GOD 80

CHAPTER EIGHT....RESTORATIONS FROM DEATH 100

CHAPTER NINE....HEALING 111

CHAPTER TEN...PROSPERITY 121

BECOMING A CHRISTIAN 142

INTRODUCTION

The Word of God emphasises the need to eradicate every form of premature death in our midst by writing in the Bible that the last enemy that shall be defeated is death itself and the fear of death.

> The last enemy to be
> subdued and abolished is death
>
> (1 Corinthians 15:26)

For God to have written in the Bible the necessity to terminate and abolished death, that shows that the study (this book) about the subject that "there is no death in Christ" is very essential. I encourage someone to be willing to fight the good fight of faith by cooperating with the Spirit of The Living God through The Word of God to conquer the fear of death.

In this book, someone will understand the full meaning of the covenant of salvation they have in Christ Jesus. They will understand that being a Christian is more than a tradition, it is a covenant of Long Living, full life and life in abundant. Christian

Faith is a covenant of prosperity, blessings and the Spirit of rejoicing in abundant. Christian Faith carries with it the opportunities to have some good access to all the blessings God promises in The Bible. It qualifies us to become the Joint Heirs with Jesus Christ. Our absolute trust must be in The Word of God and the anointed teachings God placed in our lives. No one should settle for anything less than The Abundant life God promises us. Long life means being healthy, wealthy, fruitful and prosperous in all good things.

God's Word says, at old age we shall still be bringing forth good fruits and not troubles in The Name of Jesus Christ. We shall not be brought forward for troubles in The Name of Jesus Christ.

> [Growing in grace] they shall still
> bring forth fruit in old age; they shall
> be full of sap [of spiritual vitality] and
> [rich in the] verdure [of trust, love,
> and contentment] (Psalm 92:14)

The day you accepted Jesus Christ as your Lord and Saviour, what you received is the covenant that qualifies you for an abundant life, long living, healing and health, strength, joy, longevity and prosperities.

If you have prayed the prayer of salvation and have accepted Jesus Christ as your Lord and Saviour, you have a covenant with God. For your joy to abound, you need to study The Word of God and co-operate with the Holy Spirit (The Wisdom of God) concerning all things. The Holy Spirit is The Teacher and He is capable of teaching each and every one of us all things that pertains to life and Godliness.

> But the Comforter (Counsellor, Helper, Intercessor, Advocate, Strengthener, Standby), the Holy Spirit, Whom the Father will send in My name [in My place, to represent Me and act on My behalf], He will teach you all things. And He will cause you to recall (will remind you of, bring to your remembrance) everything I have told you (John 14:26)

Your covenant is a covenant of Long living and not of short living. You have a covenant for healing and not for sickness. You have a covenant to enjoy life and enjoy it to the full, you have a covenant of prosperity and freedom from poverty and all forms of embarrassing situations. In this book we shall look through the Scriptures that promises us of the Salvations we have in Christ Jesus.

As long as we tune in to The Word of God, what we shall receive will be life without end in The Name of Jesus Christ. To be successful in our Christian Journey, we must cooperate with The Spirit of The Living God and not our feelings or men's opinions that are contrary to Christ.

How do we receive the Holy Spirit? We receive The Holy Spirit from God through The Word of God. I pray that The Lord God will separate us and deliver us from anything that tries to compete with His counsels and blessings for us in The Name of Jesus Christ.

CHAPTER ONE

JESUS CHRIST IS THE LORD

Because if you
acknowledge and confess with your
lips that Jesus is Lord and in your
heart believe (adhere to, trust in, and
rely on the truth) that God raised
Him from the dead, you will be
saved (Romans 10:9)

The Word of God is simple, it is straightforward, nothing complicated about it for anyone that invest the time to build their lives on it. The Word of God is for everyone who has accepted Jesus Christ as their Lord and Saviour and for everyone who will accept Jesus Christ as their Lord and Saviour. Romans 10:9 simplify it for us that everyone who accepted Jesus Christ as their Lord and Saviour is saved. Saved from all evils, saved from sickness, saved from poverty and lack, saved from all calamities and saved from death. I would want the readers of this book to be conscious of their covenant with God The Almighty. The covenant we have with God is not a covenant of short living but that of long life and prosperities. Covenant with God through His Son Jesus Christ is the strongest covenant that anyone can come into, it is stronger than any other blood covenant which may carry with it every unnecessary penalties. The end result of the covenant with God through the blood of Jesus Christ is life eternal, forgiveness from sin and errors, it is salvation, blessings, prosperities, wisdom, joy, celebrations and long living.

> He went once for all into the [Holy of] Holies [of heaven], not by virtue of the blood of goats and calves [by which to make reconciliation between God and man], but His own blood, having found and secured a complete redemption (an everlasting release for us) (Hebrews 9:12)

It is an insult to God whenever we settle for what God has not given us, such as sickness, lack, poverty or death. The price Jesus paid is for us to receive healing, health, prosperity and life in abundance.

Everyone must be ready and be willing to protect and preserve their covenant right as Christian.

Our covenant with God is a guarantee for our salvation and redemption from all evils. God wants us to enjoy life and have life in abundant, not just to be occupying spaces and waiting to go to heaven. He want our lives to matter, relevant and precious in the sight of God and man. Therefore, God added some further conditions to our covenant with Him, the conditions that will make our lives to be blessed and become a blessing. God wants His Word, as it is in the Bible to dwell in us richly, God wants us to learn His words and to teach our children His laws.

And these words which I am commanding you this day shall be [first] in your [own] minds and hearts; [then]. You shall whet and sharpen them so as to make them penetrate, and teach and impress them diligently upon the [minds and] hearts of your children, and shall talk of them when you sit in your house and when you walk by the way, and when you lie down and when you rise up. And you shall bind them as a sign upon your hand, and they shall be as frontlets (forehead bands) between your eyes. And you shall write them upon the doorposts

7

of your house and on your gates
(Deuteronomy 6:6-9)

If you will listen diligently to the voice
of the Lord your God, being watchful
to do all His commandments which I
command you this day, the Lord
your God will set you high above all
the nations of the earth
(Deuteronomy 28:1)

God wants us to have delight in His Word, though we have covenant with God, He wants to teach us how to come into that full blessings He promised us. He wants us to give Him our ears, to listen diligently to His laws and to allow His Words to guide us into all truth. God's laws are His Words, the Bible says the commandments of the Lord are not grievous, they are not too difficult to reach and to obey, and God's yoke is easy to bear. For the Word of God to be at our reach always, He has set some men and women apart to study and listen to His Words so as to write them down for us and to teach us. Now it is up to individual to choose life by choosing to listen to The Word of God and to obey them.

For this commandment which I command you this day is not too difficult for you, nor is it far off. It is not [a secret laid up] in heaven, that you should say, Who shall go up for us to heaven and bring it to us, that we may hear and do it? Neither is it beyond the sea, that you should say, Who shall go over the sea for us and bring it to us, that we may hear and do it? **But the word is very near you, in your mouth and in your mind and in your heart, so that you can do it** (Deuteronomy 30:11-14)

The Word of God is not too far, there is no nation, city or town where people do not have access to The Living Word of God in all various forms of format. The Word of God is available these days in audio and visual formats. God desires for everyone to set time apart to honour Him by choosing to study His Word.

What God is saying to us is that His commandments are not too difficult, if there is any part of the commandment of the Lord that seems difficult for us to obey, I will advise that we make it our area of specialisation to study. We should study every literatures and the teachings available for that particular topic until God give us the total victory over the situation. We should ask The Lord to give us The Wisdom necessary to gain mastery over every situation in The Name of Jesus Christ. We should make it our ambition to study the particular subject very well and if possible, do some research on it, we should pray and trust that God will empower us to overcome all temptations in The Name of Jesus Christ. He will empower each and every one of us by releasing the light of His Word to penetrate the situations we may be facing until we become an overcomer in that particular area, until God terminate every wrong spirits for our sake in The Name of Jesus Christ. May I advise that we study other Christian leaders literatures and teachings as well, and allow the Word of God to minister to us.

The Sincerity of The Word of God

Every Christian must have the good knowledge of what it means to be a Christian, especially, the born again Christians. Romans 10:9 must be a good anchor for every Christian to hold unto "that if you confess by accepting Jesus Christ as your Lord and Saviour, you are saved". The Word of God is sincere, there is no error in it. God wants us to enjoy the covenant of salvation in all the areas of our lives by making sure that His Living Word dwells in us richly. For us to blossom for God, we need to then seek the face of God through His Words to find out more deeply what God required from us to do to come into the abundant life He promised us.

The commandments of The Lord is not too difficult to obey. All the commandments of The Lord can be found in The Holy Bible, the Bible is The Word of God. Learning from all the patriarchs of faith in the Bible and the Wisdom of God in The Bible will definitely launch anyone into the blessings of The Lord God for them. There is no other short cut to being blessed or to receive from God apart from His Word, everyone must choose to study The Bible and found out what God is saying concerning a particular situation they are facing. The Bible says God is no respecter of persons, He is the same God over all. He promised His blessings on all that choose to believe in Him, both for the high and the lowly (Psalm 133:3) Amp. God wants our lives to matter, He wants us to be relevant and to manifest His blessings in the land of the living, and how to achieve that is by allowing The Wisdom of God to guide us.

Becoming a Good Witness for God

Oh, that men would praise [and
confess to] the Lord for His

goodness and loving-kindness and His wonderful works to the children of men! And let them sacrifice the sacrifices of thanksgiving and rehearse His deeds with shouts of joy and singing! (Psalm 107: 21-22)

It delights God whenever we confess what He says, none of us will be glad if someone is going about telling lies against us. God wants His Children to be familiar with His language. He wants us to say what He says by becoming a good witness for Him, by testifying of God's goodness in the land of the living. Jesus Christ must be our good example to emulate by choosing to say what The Father God says. There is power in what we says continually. I pray that The Lord God will empower us to confess His faithfulness to us and to humanity. I pray that no negative situations or voices will be able to change our perspective of God to evils in The Name of Jesus Christ.

No corrupt and wrong communications shall emerge from us in The Name of Jesus Christ. God will empower us to say what He says in The Name of Jesus Christ and not what our feelings and circumstances is dictating to us. The Bible says that the power of life and death is in the tongue (Proverbs 18:21) May I advise the readers of this book to cultivate the habit of declaring the goodness of The Lord concerning everything that pertain to them, to say what God says in The Bible regularly. God wants us to learn His laws when we are still young (meaning now), believing that when we are old we shall not depart from the sound doctrine. He wants us to teach it to our children. He wants us to enjoy life and have life more abundantly. There is power in what we say continually. We must trained our spirit, soul and body to only declare what God says concerning us.

Your word have I laid up in my heart, that I might not sin against You (Psalm 119:11)

For whatever is born of God is victorious over the world; and this is the victory that conquers the world, even our faith. Who is it that is victorious over [that conquers] the world but he who believes that Jesus is the Son of God [who adheres to, trusts in, and relies on that fact]? This is He Who came by (with) water and blood [His baptism and His death], Jesus Christ (the Messiah)— not by (in) the water only, but by (in) the water and the blood. And it is the [Holy] Spirit Who bears witness, because **the [Holy] Spirit is the Truth**. So there are three witnesses in heaven: the Father, the Word and the Holy Spirit, and these three are One; and there are three witnesses on the earth: the Spirit, the water, and the blood; and these three agree [are in unison; their testimony coincides] (1 John 5: 4-8)

You Already Have Eternal Life: God is Not a Liar

Each time we doubt The Word of God, what satan is trying to achieve is for us to call God a liar, the Bible wrote that people will perish due to lack of knowledge. I pray that none of us shall perish due to the lack of knowledge in The Name of Jesus Christ. The Word of God is God, each time we doubt God, what satan is trying to tell us is that God is not in existence. God wrote in The Bible that Jesus Christ is alive, He paid the price for us to have life and to enjoy life in abundant, anything shorter than the blessings of The Lord is not from God. We must take our stand to be willing to receive in full the blessings The Lord God promised us. If we believe God for our healing, we must accept the truth that God is Our Provider. We must not give anything the authority to cut our lives and the blessings of The Lord in our lives short.

He who believes in the Son of God [who adheres to, trusts in, and relies on Him] has the testimony [possesses this divine attestation] within himself. **He who does not believe God [in this way] has made Him out to be and represented Him as a liar**, because he has not believed (put his faith in, adhered to, and relied on) the evidence (the testimony) that God has borne regarding His Son. And this is that testimony (that evidence): God gave us eternal life, and this life is in His Son. He who possesses the Son has that life; he who does not possess the Son of God does not have that life. **I write this to you who believe** in (adhere to, trust in, and rely on) the name of the Son of God [in the peculiar services and blessings conferred by Him on men], so that you may know [with settled and absolute knowledge] that **you [already] have life, yes, eternal life** (1 John 5: 10-13)

Each time we are ignorant of the truth of The Word of God, what satan is doing to us is to make the world to see God as a liar, God is not a liar, in God is all the truth we will ever need to live a victorious life. If God can testify that Jesus Christ is alive (the Spirit of God in us), then it will be wrong to believe anything different. For God so love the world and He put all His laws and blessings into writing for those who believe in Him so that we will not forget our inheritance of salvation in Him.

Our salvation in Christ is not what we have to beg someone to give to us, neither is it something we have to be running from pole to pillars always to seek. If you believe in Jesus Christ and have good trust in The Word of God, you have eternal life already. All you have to do is to believe all The Good Promises of God in The Bible for you. Eternal life is life without end, it is having the life that is in Christ Jesus. It is to be able to have your bills paid and have all your needs met. The Bible says that as Christ is, so we are. And how is Christ? He is alive, He is not in the grave, He is seating at the right hand of The Father God making intercessions for us.

You do not need anyone to come and approve your being alive, you don't need any man with known titles or unknown titles to come and approve whether you should live or not. Get into the Word of God and consume good dosage of the Word of

God. Allow The Word of God to flush away from you every wrong thinking's in The Name of Jesus Christ.

> God is not a man that He should
> tell or act a lie, neither the son of
> man, that He should feel
> repentance or compunction [for what
> He has promised]. Has He said and
> shall He not do it? Or has He spoken
> and shall He not make it good?
> (Numbers 23:19)

Who Has Your Ears

Give your ears to The Word of God and not to every news and the gossips in the town.

It is insulting whenever we allow the opinion of men or our feelings to gain more grounds in our lives than that of God. Do not allow anything or anyone to distract your attention from The Word of God, especially, from your personal devotion times with God. Everywhere in the Bible, God says pay attention to my Word, He never says pay attention to your feelings or to the people's opinion about you. And you can cast down every imagination and every thoughts that tries to exalt itself above the Wisdom of God in your life. The Word of God must have greater authority over us than the Word of men.

> If we accept [as we do] the testimony of men [if we are willing to take human authority], the testimony of God is greater (of stronger authority), for this is the testimony of God, even the witness which He has borne regarding His Son (1 John 5: 9)

God Himself bear the witness that His Son is alive and He is dependable, anything shorter than that is a way to annul The Truth of The Word of God and our salvation in Christ, that will not happen to us and it will not be our portion in The Name of Jesus Christ.

God is not saying we should not honour the authority, but where the authority is about to miss the mark or where they are about to miss their good purposes, we can pray to God to align them with His good purposes for them and for us. If you are ignorant of the Word of God, you may not know what to pray about or what actions to take in the seasons of challenges, but where The Wisdom of God dwells, there is freedom from all forms of pain and confusions. Authorities has been put there to manifest the purpose of God, for there is no authority without God (see Romans 13:1) Our good knowledge of The Word of God will not make it possible for anyone or any institutions to manipulate us, rather, God can use us to minister grace to the authorities in The Name of Jesus Christ.

> Let him who receives instruction in
> the Word [of God] share all good
> things with his teacher [contributing
> to his support] (Galatians 6:6)

Good knowledge of the Word of God will empowers us to be good citizens, it will empowers us to carry out our duties according to the Will of God.

Where there is lack of knowledge, people perish, I pray that no one will perish due to lack of knowledge in The Name of Jesus Christ. I pray that no one will go about confessing what God has not confess about their situations, Proverbs 4:24 calls it a dishonest speech whenever we say what God has not says. We are advised to put away from us every wilful and contrary talk, both the ones generated by ourselves and the ones from any institutions. We should fix our minds on the promises and the blessings of The Lord, not on the wrong reports from any institutions or from anyone.

Fixing our minds on the Word of God can save us from our feelings and emotions which can change at any time. It can deliver us from what the Bible calls the wicked spirit.

My son, attend to my words;
consent and submit to my sayings.
Let them not depart from your sight;
keep them in the centre of your
heart. For they are life to those who
find them, healing and health to all
their flesh. Keep and guard your
heart with all vigilance and above all
that you guard, for out of it flow the
springs of life. Put away from you
false and dishonest speech, and
willful and contrary talk put far from
you. Let your eyes look right on [with
fixed purpose], and let your gaze be
straight before you. Consider well
the path of your feet, and let all your
ways be established and ordered
aright. Turn not aside to the right
hand or to the left; remove your foot
from evil (Proverbs 4: 20-27)

Consider well the path of your feet, receive God's direction for all your journey, not everywhere you should always go, listen to what God will have to say concerning all situations.

Paying attention to the Word of God is the best way to submit our feelings and every ungodly desires to God. It is a way to receive the quality lifestyle God promised us. It is a way to exchange our little thinking and every ungodly character to God's superior lifestyle. It is a way not to be craving for the base, dry, lack of joy lifestyles that satan plans to dish out for us.

Blessed (happy, fortunate, prosperous, and enviable) is the man who walks and lives not in the counsel of the ungodly [following their advice, their plans and purposes], nor stands [submissive and inactive] in the path where sinners walk, nor sits down [to relax and rest] where the scornful [and the mockers] gather. But his delight and desire are in the law of the Lord, and on His law (the precepts, the instructions, the teachings of God) he habitually meditates (ponders and studies) by day and by night. And he shall be like a tree firmly planted [and tended] by the streams of water,

21

ready to bring forth its fruit in its
season; its leaf also shall not
fade or wither; and everything he
does shall prosper [and come to
maturity] (Psalm 1: 1-3)

To be truly well, strong and healthy, we must all crave for the Word of God, we must avoid every unhealthy conversations and refuse to be engaged with all kinds of wrong controversies. The Bible says that God will judge us concerning every non profitable, idle jesting's we get ourselves into in the day of judgement, therefore we must avoid all kinds of wrong conversations that doesn't bless us or anyone except the devil. I will advise the readers of this book not to wait till the day of judgement, they should make it their habit to acquaint themselves with the Word of God from now and it will bring healing and health to all their flesh and bones in The Name of Jesus Christ.

CHAPTER TWO

PUTTING ON THE IMMORTALITY

For this perishable [part of us] must
put on the imperishable [nature], and
this mortal [part of us, this nature
that is capable of dying] must put on
immortality (freedom from death) (1
Corinthians 15:53)

The Bible advices that we must all be born again by
confessing Jesus Christ as our Lord and Saviour.
For us to be healthy and start enjoying life to the
full, we then needs to put on the Word of God by
receiving it into our spirit, soul and body. The Word
of God is a Living Word, it is active, and it has
power and life in it to preserve life from death and
decay. The Bible says that the Word of God is
capable of renewing our life and strength better
than that of the eagles (see Psalm 103:5)

Marvel not [do not be surprised,
astonished] at My telling you, You
must all be born anew (from above)
(John 3:7)

Being born again from above means receiving the
Word of God and allowed the invincible God to give
you new life which has no ending.

Just a little while now, and the world
will not see Me any more, but you
will see Me; because I live, you will
live also (John 14:19)

Anyone that is born again lives in the realm where
God dwells, those that are not born again may not
understand what it means to live in a different realm
from them. As you constantly allow the Word of God
to teach you all things, as you constantly opens
your eyes and ears to receive the Word of God, you
will develop a good relationship with God and the
Word of God shall become a Living Word in you
and for you. As Christians, once you start
developing your faith through the Word of God, the
Word of God will teach you all things and you will
see God continually through His Word. You will
abide with God and His principles and not only on

24

what your feeling and flesh dictates to you. The Word of God shall deliver you from all kinds of evils that cut lives short in the Name of Jesus Christ. The Word of God will releases unto you the ability to rejoices, to be healthy, wealthy and prosperous. Your lifestyle will improve as much as you continue to listen to what God will say to you. As you pay attention to The Word of God and obey, the blessings will overtake you and comes to you abundantly in The Name of Jesus Christ. Paying attention to The Promises of God as it is in the Bible is the only thing beneficiary to us.

Good praise and worship, sincere praise and worship, from the heart unto The Father God is a good way to put on God. As we develop the good habit of rejoicing at the presence of God, nations will see the joy and the blessings of the Lord around us. Demons will flee from us, satan will not be able to take over our lives and our land, sickness and death shall have no spaces in The Name of Jesus Christ. Every wrong spirits shall see that their schemes is not working, they will not come near our dwelling places, because they will see that we are healthy, wealthy and wise in The Name of Jesus Christ.

You Have a Role to Play

Jesus Christ paid the price already for our total salvation, for that salvation to last long, for you to move from the realm of struggling for any good things, for you not to just occupy space till Christ comes, for you not to beg for bread at any point in time, you have to be ready to fight the good fight of faith by choosing to pay more attention to The Word of God, by giving unto God the Praise and Worship that is due to Him, by being joyful through the spirit of The Living God, by making the conscious efforts to choose to be well even when everything seems to be against you, by asking The Lord God to order your steps everywhere you go. By choosing to do Gods bidding while you are on this planet earth, by choosing to work with The Father God, by being constant in prayer, praying according to The Word of God. The more you choose to work with God, the more you are busy with God, the more you will discover God's perfect will for your life, the more He will bless you, the more you will manifest His blessings in The Name of Jesus Christ.

Pray For Your Family, Friends and Those in Positions of Authority Regularly

First of all, then, I
admonish and urge that petitions,

prayers, intercessions, and
thanksgivings be offered on behalf of
all men. For kings and all who are in
positions of authority or high
responsibility, that [outwardly] we
may pass a quiet and undisturbed
life [and inwardly] a peaceable one
in all godliness and reverence and
seriousness in every way.

(1 Timothy 2: 1-2)

As Christians, we are saved from all evils, known
and unknown, for us to truly enjoy the abundant life
God promises us, the Bible advices that we should
pray for our family, friends, kings and everyone in
positions of authority. For those in positions of
authority to make precise Godly decisions that will
bless us.

For such [praying] is good and right,
and [it is] pleasing and acceptable to
God our Saviour. Who wishes all
men to be saved and [increasingly]
to perceive and recognize and
discern and know
precisely and correctly the [divine]
Truth (1 Timothy 2: 3-4)

We are to pray for those in positions of authorities such as the political leaders, the monarch, the education sectors, business sectors, health departments, churches and every souls everywhere for the Wisdom of God to fill each and every one of us and to guide us in all our decision making.

You will not catch death, sickness, poverty or lack if your mind, spirit, soul and body is constantly working with God.

Praying for others is working for God and the Bible says that God shall reward us for every good works, and that our labour of love shall not be in vain.

We are to pray for the Wisdom of God to enter into and direct everyone God placed in our lives, especially those whose decisions may affect our own decisions. Such prayers is capable of preventing us from being deceived and misled by any companionship. In other for us not to fall into wrong counsels, we must be fervent in spirit serving the Lord. Wrong counsels can come from anywhere, hence the reason why we must obey the Word of God by choosing to stand in the gap for our family, friends, government and every institutions in our land so that satan will not have authority over those we trust. The Bible says that we wrestle not against flesh and blood, but against every wicked spirit in the spiritual realms (Ephesians 6:12).

Our obedience to The Word of God will not allow evils to manifest itself in our land, our busyness with God will only give us long life and prosperity in The Name of Jesus Christ.

You can stand in the gap and asked The Lord God to silent every wrong laws, wrong bills, wrong voices, wrong judgements, wrong counsels for your sake in The Name of Jesus Christ.

> Do not be so deceived and misled!
> Evil companionships (communion, associations) corrupt and deprave good
> manners and morals and character
> (1 Corinthians 15: 33)

The Word of God is big enough to mould our characters and that of those around us, it is capable of making our covenant with God to stand and last beyond eternity. Our covenant of longevity will endure more as we choose to love The Word of God and live by its principles. It must get to a season in our lives when unnecessary conversations doesn't interest us anymore. If any conversation does not align with the Word of God, if it will not bless us, we should not waste our time on them and we should not engage ourselves with every wrong conversations.

We do not need to go and inform those we prayed for that we are praying for them all the time, we should make it our profession to keep doing good, knowing that for every good seed of obedience to the will of God, our good reward and harvest times shall come in The Name of Jesus Christ. I pray that none of us will have any reason to stop doing good for any reason in the Name of Jesus Christ.

Therefore, my beloved brethren, be firm (steadfast), immovable, always abounding in the work of the Lord [always being superior, excelling, doing more than enough in the service of the Lord], knowing and being continually aware that your labour in the Lord is not futile [it is never wasted or to no purpose] (1 Corinthians 15:58)

Each time we choose to do things God's way by choosing to do good, God is giving us the opportunity to show our superiority over satan and its kingdom by raising standard against the works of satan. Our action and attitudes should always be superior to that of satan always.

Receiving The Word of God in abundant, praying according to the will of God and having a good expectations towards one another shall definitely help us to eradicate evils in our lands in The Name of Jesus Christ. When we show kindness to someone and let go of all forms of grievances, when we allowed the Holy Spirit to fill us, we are adding more good spiritual nutrients to our lives. The acts of kindness, the acts of not storing up offences in our spirit, soul and body will help us to enjoy life more in abundance. I pray that the Holy Spirit will empower us to be able to receive the good lifestyle Jesus paid for us to have in The Name of Jesus Christ.

The day we accept Jesus Christ as our Lord and Saviour and starts to study The Word of God was and is the day we switched lane from death to life. As long as we continue to receive our spiritual nutrients from the Word of God, satan can never have authority over us, Jesus Christ has annulled death on our behalf. The Word of God will renew our lives as we continue in it in The Name of Jesus Christ.

[It is that purpose and grace] which
He now has made known and has
fully disclosed and made real [to us]
through the appearing of our Saviour

Christ Jesus, Who annulled
death and made it of no effect and
brought life and immortality
(immunity from eternal death) to light
through the Gospel (2 Timothy 1:10)

But God Raised Him from the Dead

Satan, death, sickness and lack do not have power over humanity, satan only has power as much as each individual give him authority over them. And God did not give any human being the authority to kill each other, we should not be the one who approved anyone to speak death over our lives in The Name of Jesus Christ. Your boss at work should only pronounce blessings over you and not death.

Say This Out Loud

No one has authority to pronounce death over me in The Name of Jesus Christ as I cooperate with The Word of God to bless me. As I choose to honour God and His Words, infinite life is my inheritance in The Name of Jesus Christ. I choose to chase God and not man. I choose to seek the Wisdom and the kingdom of God first and every other things shall be added unto me in The Name of Jesus Christ. The Word of God will teach me how to honour my leaders and those in positions of authority, and as I obey The Lord, His blessings shall rest on my life and everything that belongs to me in The Name of Jesus Christ. The Word of God shall be the centre of my focus, it shall teach me all things. It shall save me and everything that belongs to me in The Name of Jesus Christ. As I choose to relate with my brothers and sisters in Christ, no weapons formed by satan against each and every one of us shall prosper in The Name of Jesus Christ. No weapons formed by satan against the body of Christ shall prosper in The Name of Jesus Christ.

Learn From the Ministry of Jesus

Jesus did not cooperate with anything that is contrary to the will of God throughout His earthly ministry and even after:

Instances from The Bible:

1. Jesus Christ refused to cooperate with satan after Jesus fasted for forty days without food and water and He was hungry, Jesus nullified every suggestions that satan threw at Him (Matthew 4)
2. Jesus Christ refused to cooperate with the situations and the disciples that there was a shortage of food to feed the five thousand

souls that were with Him. He refused to send them away, He refused to call the place and their space a barren place and He refused to say that the day of their fellowship together was over (Matthew 14: 15-21). If any situation is trying to present itself to you the way that is contrary to Christ, say to the situation that it has no final say in your life. The Word of God is the authority in The Name of Jesus Christ. Declare and decree the Word of God concerning your life and the lives of your loved ones, not what satan and the situations is dictating to you.

3. Another story where Jesus taught us how not to cooperate with evil is in the story of Lazarus. Jesus declared the result He expected, and that is what He received by saying "This sickness is not to end in death". I pray that The Holy Spirit of The Living God will enter into each and every one of us and terminate every evil imaginations in The Name of Jesus Christ ((John 11: 1-45)

4. The story of Jairus daughter is a good example of where Jesus annulled death. Jesus refused to cooperate with satan and death concerning Jairus daughter. Jesus Christ advised Jairus to ignore the words of men but to believe in God. And as Jairus trusted God the Father through The Word of

Jesus Christ, his daughter came back to life (Luke 8: 40-56)

Whatever may be your need today, trust God and His Words, and He shall bring it to reality in the Name of Jesus Christ. No evils shall become reality in your life in The Name of Jesus Christ.

Jesus Christ proved that God's Word is the final authority concerning all things and not the opinion of men, not what the circumstances is dictating, not your feelings, not your bank accounts, not your imaginations, but only The Truth of The Word of God.

Concerning all things, allow the Word of God to be the authority and not the voice from anyone. As you continue to be steadfast in the Word of God, as you continue to stand firm on the Word of God, you shall see its good manifestations in The Name of Jesus Christ.

We thank God for His mercy over humanity, we thank God who will look beyond faults and still save souls. We thank God for He has power over sickness, lack, death and every unpleasant situations. The Christian faith we received is not a dead religion. The Bible says, as Christ is, so we are, and how is Christ? He is alive, He is not in the grave. The Bible testifies to Christ's resurrection and His disciples testify also.

But God raised Him from the dead
(Acts 13:30)

Strive to Enter Through the Narrow Gate

And he who does not take up his
cross and follow Me [cleave
steadfastly to Me, conforming wholly
to My example in living and, if need
be, in dying also] is not worthy of
Me. Whoever finds his [lower] life will
lose it [the higher life], and whoever
loses his [lower] life on My account
will find it [the higher life] (Matthew
10:38-39)

Dying mentioned in the book of Matthew 10:38 is dying to some habits that are not of God, dying to the carnal nature and allow the Word of God to be The Master.

Every enjoyment that is only for immediate gratifications only without any future benefit is called the lower life (low quality lifestyle), that is not what we should be seeking always. We should strive for what has eternal values by choosing to study the Word of God (see Proverbs 3: 1-2 and 2 Timothy 2:

15) We must all be willing to go through some hardship and delay some enjoyments if possible for us to enter and enjoy the best life God has for us. We should always pray to God to empower us to endure, to always wait on Him for the blessings, not for the punishment, shame or reproach. We must trust and know that God's plans for us will always be good and not evil. Our rewards shall not be evil in The Name of Jesus Christ.

Matthew 10: 38 encourages us to be willing to delay some enjoyments, to be willing to die to some cravings (the sensual nature), to carry our cross by receiving our responsibilities to serve God and follow His ways. Then we will find the higher life (the superior lifestyle) with no lack, no sickness, no shame or death in The Name of Jesus Christ.

God Will Not Allow His Holy Ones to See Corruptions

So now we are bringing you the good news (Gospel) that what God promised to our forefathers. This He has completely fulfilled for us, their children, by raising up Jesus, as it is written in the second psalm, You are My Son; today I have begotten You [caused You to arise, to be born; formally shown You to be the Messiah by the resurrection] (Psalm 2:7) And as to His having raised Him from among the dead, **now no more to return to [undergo] putrefaction and dissolution [of the grave],** He spoke in this way, I will fulfil and give to you the holy and sure mercy and blessings [that were promised and assured] to David. For this reason He says also in another psalm, You will not allow Your Holy One to see corruption [to undergo putrefaction and dissolution of the grave] (Acts 13: 32-35,)

For You will not abandon me to Sheol (the place of the dead), neither will You suffer Your holy one [Holy One] to see corruption (Psalm 16:10)

Incline your ear [submit and consent to the divine will] and come to Me; hear, and your soul will revive; and I will make an everlasting covenant or league with you, even the sure mercy (kindness, goodwill, and compassion) promised to David (Isaiah 55:3)

God gave to us His promises in His Word that He will not allow us to see corruption and every dishonest proceedings which leads to death. We too must be very conscious to avoid every act of dishonesty and to pray and ask for God's divine protection always from every form of temptations, to resist the devil until it flees from us in The Name of Jesus Christ. The way to resist and conquers evil is to choose to drink from the fountains of The Word of God, by preferring the Word of God compared to every other things.

CHAPTER THREE

THE WHOLE ARMOUR OF GOD

Put on God's whole armour [the
armour of a heavy-armed soldier
which God supplies], that you may
be able successfully to stand up
against [all] the strategies and the
deceits of the devil (Ephesians 6:11)

Putting on the Armour of God means accepting the
Word of God fully, it means to become the lifetime
student of The Word of God. Each time we study
the Word of God, we put on God, we wear God by
receiving His Spirit into our spirit. There is no part of
The Bible that is not good. Form Genesis to
Revelation, what you and I will learn are the
essential ingredients to make us blossom for God.
Therefore, we all need to study The Bible and every
other Christian Literature on a daily basis and apply
all its good principles into our lives.

The Bible advises us to put on The Word of God
because it is capable of making us to withstand and

expels all the strategies, plans and the schemes of satan. No soldier will go into practice in the time of war, for any soldier to conquer during the war, they have to set time apart to train and be prepared before they see any signs of war at all. So God is advising His Children to be wise by being prepared against the storm the live may send their ways. To be ready to stand their grounds at all times.

Therefore put on God's **complete**
armour, that you may be able to
resist and stand your ground on the
evil day [of danger], and, having
done all [the crisis demands], to
stand [firmly in your place]
(Ephesians 6: 13)

The Word of God is the Armour of God

In the beginning [before all time] was
the Word (Christ), and the Word was
with God, and the Word was
God Himself (John 1:1)

He sends forth His word and heals
them and rescues them from the
pit and destruction (Psalm 107:20)

Whenever God wants to save anyone, He always send them His Words which is capable of delivering anyone from danger. From Genesis to Revelation, God emphasises that we must attend to His Word, in the presence of God is the fullness of joy. I pray that no one shall be afflicted by satan from where God planted them by the river side of His Word in The Name of Jesus Christ.

Praise and Worship is the Armour of God

But You are holy, O You Who dwell
in [the holy place where] the praises
of Israel [are offered] (Psalm 22:3)

God inhabits the praises of His people, both the corporate worship and the personal worship moments are all welcomed by the Father God. The Spirit of The Living God tends to tabernacle where people sing praises unto the Lord and not where there is passivity and lack of joy. There is tends to be more increase in productivity of every good works where people are well and are in good spirit, hence God encourages us to create an atmosphere where He can come and minister to our needs by releasing some good flavour of praise and worship unto Him.

I pray that whenever heavens look at us, our lives will not be full of request for material properties and possessions only, but we shall be full of praises unto our God because we shall be surrounded by the evidence of God's blessings in our lives in The Name of Jesus Christ. Our generation shall be known for rejoicing always, because the spirit of sadness shall no longer be our portions in The Name of Jesus Christ.

> But you are a chosen race, a royal priesthood, a dedicated nation, [God's] own purchased, special people, that you may set forth the wonderful deeds and display the virtues and perfections of Him Who called you out of darkness into His marvellous light (1 Peter 2:9)

Curse shall no longer be our portions because our songs shall be, "forever praising God for His faithfulness", not scolding God for all His faithfulness to us. We shall be able to think and look around us and have millions of reasons to praise God always. There is a saying that if you know how to think, you will know how to thank God.

May God not says concerning us the only thing we know how to do is to bombard heavens with our prayer request and shopping list always. Rather heaven will supply our needs abundantly because of our good attitudes towards God, because we know how to say thank You Lord. May God be pleased with us always in The Name of Jesus Christ. May our good attitudes extends to those God placed and will place in our lives. We shall not be a target for destructions in The Name of Jesus Christ. No weapons formed by satan shall have authority over us in The Name of Jesus Christ. May God never says concerning us that we do not know how to give but to take. May heaven equipped us and prepared us to be able to give good gifts in The Name of Jesus Christ.

You have not bought Me sweet cane with money, or satiated Me with the fat of your sacrifices. But you have only burdened Me with your sins; you have wearied Me with your iniquities (Isaiah 43: 24)

Prayer

Do not fret or have any anxiety about anything, but in every

circumstance and in everything, by
prayer and petition (definite
requests), **with thanksgiving**,
continue to make your wants known
to God (Philippians 4:6)

Lord, thank You for giving unto us good and Godly Spirit, thank You for creating in us good heart of gratitude to praise You for who You are, for all the prices You have paid on our behalf. Thank You for giving unto us Your Holy Spirit.

We must never forget the attitude of worship, we must never forget the attitudes of giving all praises unto God. We must praise God in an anticipation of His blessings that will come to us.

Prayer is a Good Armour of God

And the prayer [that is] of faith will
save him who is sick, and the Lord
will restore him; and if he has
committed sins, he will be forgiven
(James 5:15)

.....The earnest (heartfelt, continued)
prayer of a righteous man makes
tremendous power available

[dynamic in its working (James 5:
16c)

Our prayers must be based on The Word of God,
not what we think in our mind only, and God will
fulfil every expectations that is according to His Will.
We must pray into existence the blessings we see
in The Word of God.

Studying the Word of God is a good way to put on
the armour of God. Staying under a good anointed
teaching of The Word of God is a good way to put
on the Armour of God. Putting on the Armour of
God has some good rewards for us, we must crave
for the Word of God. We must love The Word of
God, we must obey The Word of God and we must
teach our children to do the same. We must choose
to study The Bible from Genesis to Revelation and
all other Christian Literatures God gives to us. I pray
that The Lord God will empowers us and
encourages us to love His Word and to choose to
study them.

And this is the confidence (the
assurance, the privilege of boldness)
which we have in Him: [we are sure]
that if we ask anything (make any
request) according to His will (in

47

agreement with His own plan), He
listens to and hears us (1 John 5:14)

There is a great rewards for everyone who have
accepted Jesus Christ as their Lord and Saviour.
Christian Faith is a faith of covenant with God, it is a
covenant that promises us longevity. The blessings
of The Lord, it makes riches without adding sorrow
unto it.

Right from inception satan has been trying to
deceived and deviate humanity by luring them into
all kinds of evils, but despite all satans strategies,
God always comes through for His people.

There is no death for everyone who has confessed
Jesus Christ as their Lord and Saviour and choose
to cling to The Word of God. The day we confess
Jesus Christ as our Lord and Saviour was the day
we moved from death to life. Opening the book of
The Wisdom of God (The Bible) to receive your
blessings is what you have to do for yourself. Your
Bible teachers will help you if you make an efforts to
go to them and listen to them, but they may not be
able to teach you everything you needs to know.
The time should come when you have grown and
contribute to the needs of the saints spiritually and
financially because of the wealth of the Wisdom that
dwells within you.

Because if you
acknowledge and confess with your
lips that Jesus is Lord and in your
heart believe (adhere to, trust in, and
rely on the truth) that God raised
Him from the dead, you will be
saved (Romans 10:9)

CHAPTER FOUR

THE POWER OF CONTINUITY

Dwell in Me, and I will dwell in you.
[Live in Me, and I will live in you.]
Just as no branch can bear fruit of
itself without abiding in (being vitally
united to) the vine, neither can you
bear fruit unless you abide in Me
(John 15:4)

Every noise around you will tries to bid for your attentions, especially the noises that will not lead you anywhere. You are the one who will make the conscious efforts to make sure that your relationship with God is your priority. You are the one who will make the efforts to break yourself free from every spirit that tries to make slaves out of you. By constantly studying the Word of God, everything contrary to Christ shall be stripped away from us in The Name of Jesus Christ.

Marta cried out to our Lord and Saviour Jesus Christ on His visit to her house sometimes ago "Master tell my sister to help me"

But Martha [overly occupied and too busy] was distracted with much serving; and she came up to Him and said, Lord, is it nothing to You that my sister has left me to serve alone? Tell her then to help me [to lend a hand and do her part along with me]! But the Lord replied to her by saying, Martha, Martha, you are anxious and troubled about many things. There is need of only one or but a few things. Mary has chosen the good portion [that which is to her advantage], which shall not be taken away from her (Luke 10: 40-42

Nothing is wrong in lending an helping hands to someone, in fact the Bible commands it, but if only serving is about to become our culture, traditions and the only act of faith we desired to exercise. We must then come to a point of repentance to create time to listen to what The Word of God will say concerning us. We must set time apart from our overly busy lifestyles to listen to what God will have to say concerning our life and the lives of those around us. We must not be too busy with our job and not having time to listen to God. If your tradition and culture has always been looking for money, busy wanting to get something all your life, repent and combine your getting's with The Word of God and allow God to teach you how to be truly prosperous in all things.

Jesus Christ Himself promised us Infinite Life as long as we continue with Him. Our faith with Him and in Him is not what we give up on, as long as we choose to abide in the Vine (Jesus Christ). We shall continue to receive the necessary nourishments for all our needs physically, spiritually, emotionally and financially. We must not allow anything or anyone to detach us from the Word of God, our connections to The Word of God must be intact always.

Our jobs or vocations must not separate us from the love of God in Christ Jesus. Jesus Christ is The Resurrection and The Life, whoever has Christ shall not die but live, and if they die by giving up on anything that is not Godly, the end result shall be live. The only death allowed as Christian is when evil and death itself dies for our sakes, when we turn and repent from every wrong doings and pursuits and turn unto God through His Words. Jesus Christ is saying to us that, if we depart from doing evil, our reward will be good and not evil. The only death allowed is when evils dies for our sakes, when we say no to satan and all its works, when we walked away from all evils,it actually means crossing over from death to live, whenever we give up on anything that is not Godly and start receiving The Word of God. This is the reason why Jesus said, even though those that believe and have their trust in Christ dies by giving up on any evils, the result will be good and abundant life for them in this life and in the ones to come in The Name of Jesus Christ. The only death is when sickness, poverty, lack and death dies in our lives in order for us to start receive healing, health, prosperity and life without end in this life and in the one to come. Our freedom and assurance of the salvation in Christ is not the licences for us to start toying with sin or anything that can cause us any harms. It is for us do away with evil completely, to say no to satan and all its works, that is what Jesus meant when He says whoever clings to Him shall not die at all. I hope this explanations clarifies John 11: 25-26.

Whoever has received Jesus Christ and continue to allow the Word of God to dwell in them can never die, because The Word of God is Living, the Word of God is current and not passive. All the promises of God in The Bible are Active, the Word of God is capable of giving life unto any good situations.

Jesus said to her, I am [Myself] the Resurrection and the Life. Whoever believes in (adheres to, trusts in, and relies on) Me, although he may die, yet he shall live. And whoever continues to live and believes in (has faith in, cleaves to, and relies on) Me shall never [actually] die at all. (John 11: 25-26)

Rejoice

Believers should always rejoice in the hope we have in Christ. We should celebrate the truth that the life we have in Christ is infinite, it is immortal. We should rejoice in the truth of knowing that God will renew our youth and our strength better than that of the eagles on a daily basis. We should rejoice knowing that Christ has redeemed our lives from the pit and corruption. We should rejoice because Christ has beautifies us, and He will continue to do so in The Name of Jesus Christ. He has dignified us and crowned us with loving-kindness and tender mercy (Psalms 103: 1-5)

The Bible advices us to put on the garment of praise always, we are advised to rejoice in The Lord always trusting in the hope we have in Christ Jesus.

CHRISTIAN FAITH: THE COVENANT OF LONGETVITY

With long life will I satisfy him and
show him My salvation (Psalm
91:16)

Whenever we come forward to accept Jesus Christ as our Lord and Saviour, we must understand what it means is to have a covenant with God. Christian faith is a covenant of longevity, it is not a covenant of short life. Once you accept Jesus Christ as your Lord and Saviour, you must settle it in your mind that no one will be able to take you away from this world prematurely in The Name of Jesus Christ. You must know that all good things will come to you abundantly in The Name of Jesus Christ. Your covenant with God must become your number one priority and you must encourage your family and friends to do likewise. As Christian, it is more profitable for you to enter into marriage covenant with someone who has covenant with Jesus Christ, someone who has the referential fear of God in them, someone who love The Lord. If your spouse has no regard for God and His Laws, he or she is likely going to misuse and abuse you and the spouse that doesn't have Christ in them may abuse the relationship as well. Do not entangle yourself with any ungodly affairs either.

Psalm 91 is a good psalm to study and meditate on regularly, it has some good Godly promises for our protection and a good covenant on longevity. May I advise the readers of this book to read and study Psalm 91 regularly?

There are so many scriptures in The Bible that affirms that we are not meant to appear and just disappear from this world as if we never came. God wants our lives to matter and be relevant. We are here to enjoy the best God has for us and to make some good contributions to the world. The Bible says, we are supposed to live for a minimum of one hundred and twenty years, going strong and healthy daily.

> Then the Lord said, My Spirit shall
> not forever dwell and strive with
> man, for he also is flesh; but his
> days shall yet be 120 years
> (Genesis 6:3)

No More Weeping. No More Death

For those that choose to listen to what God will tell them diligently and choose to obey, there is no way they will catch death, and death can never catch them. The Bible says what has light got to do with darkness, what has living got to do with death. Christians who are in Christ cannot die again, because the day we accept Christ as our Lord and Saviour was the day we dropped everything that belongs to death and we moved from death to life in Christ. And the Bible says as Christ is, so we are. Christ is not in the grave, He is risen from the dead, and therefore we are joint heirs with Christ. The Bible says it pleases our Father God to give us the kingdom, therefore heaven and the earth is our inheritance. As long as we allowed the Word of God to teach us all things, it is capable of helping us to shun all evils and for all evils to flee from our presence in The Name of Jesus Christ. No evil will come near us, no danger near our dwelling places as long as we choose not to be friends with anything that belongs to the devil.

Because you have made the Lord your refuge, and the Most High your dwelling place. There shall no evil befall you, nor any plague or calamity come near your tent. For He will give His angels [especial] charge over you to accompany and defend and preserv e you in all your ways [of obedience and service] (Psalm 91: 9-11)

God will not force His will on anyone always. God wants us to grow up and learn to honour Him by accepting His Laws knowing that they are for our own benefit. If God says honour the authority, pray for them, if the authority is trying to abuse us by abusing their powers either ignorantly or knowingly. We are not the one to judge them, God says we must never cease in doing good but to overcome evils by doing good. Then God will terminate all evils for our sake, He will not allow evil to overcome us because we are obedient to God's Word.

God has never asked us to go and start fighting our own battles physically by ourselves, rather to pray for those who despitefully uses and abuse us for God to have mercy on them and turn them into His ways (see the story of Saul in Acts 9) Out of ignorant, Saul was going about persecuting the Christians, but a day came when on his way to persecute the Christians, the light from heaven flashed around him and stopped Saul from his evil deeds. God eventually pour His Holy Spirit on him and used Saul to become one of the greatest advocates for Christians. Such miracles is possible in our days if someone will choose to pray for their lands and their leaders so that satan will not have authority over them, for satan not to turn their good acts and intentions to evil.

Long Life

Long life does not mean living in abject poverty and sickness, it means being whole, intact with nothing missing, nothing broken. It means having your needs meet both spiritually and materially. It means being enjoying the best of the land. It means being the head in all good things. It means being able to get along with yourself and your neighbours. It means having an excellent spirit for all good works, it means living in the best part of the city, it means being financially buoyant. It means having good strength for all things, it means honouring the leaders and the subordinates wherever possible. These are what the Word of God meant to delivers to each and every one of us. You may say what about those who are not Christians and they all have the good things   mentioned. I will advise you to go and study their lives very well, you will see the difference that the blood of Jesus made in the lives of the believers and the unbelievers.

God's promises is for Christians to live a minimum years of one hundred and twenty, if anyone dies at one hundred, they should be count as children, because hundred year is not enough in the sight of God.

But be glad and rejoice forever in that which I create; for behold, I create Jerusalem to be a rejoicing and her people a joy. And I will rejoice in Jerusalem and be glad in My people; and the sound of weeping will no more be heard in it, nor the cry of distress.

There shall no more be in it an infant who lives but a few days, or an old man who dies prematurely; for the child shall die a hundred years old, and the sinner who dies when only a hundred years old shall be [thought only a child, cut off because he is] accursed. They shall build houses and inhabit them, and they shall plant vineyards and eat the fruit of them. They shall not build and another inhabit; they shall not plant and another eat [the fruit]. For as the days of a tree, so shall be the days of My people, and My chosen and elect shall long make use of and enjoy the work of their hands. They shall not labour in vain or bring forth [children] for sudden terror or calamity; for they shall be the descendants of the blessed of the Lord, and their offspring with

them. And it shall be that before
they call I will answer; and while they
are yet speaking I will hear (Isaiah
65: 18-24)

Our obedient to the Word of God and to the
authority will make God to keep His covenant with
us. If we choose to listen to our parents, both
biological and spiritual, it shall be well with us is
what the Bible says.

My son, attend to my words;
consent and submit to my sayings.
Let them not depart from your sight;
keep them in the centre of your
heart. For they are life to those who
find them, healing and health to all
their flesh (Proverbs 4: 20-22)

No condemnations in Christ Jesus

Therefore, [there is] now no
condemnation (no adjudging guilty of
wrong) for those who are in Christ
Jesus, who live [and] walk not after
the dictates of the flesh, but after the
dictates of the Spirit. For the law of

the Spirit of life [which is] in Christ
Jesus [the law of our new being] has
freed me from the law of sin and of
death (Romans 8:1-2)

Christ Himself carried our guilt and our penalty so
that we do not have to carry them again. The
chastisement for our peace was laid on Him. For
everyone who has repented from their sin and
turned towards receiving The Word of God, the
Bible says they cannot be condemned to death or
destructions. The Spirit of life in Christ Jesus
immunise us from the spirit of death. I pray that The
Lord God will grant each and every one of us the
grace to love Him and to love His Laws in The
Name of Jesus Christ.

He was despised and
rejected and forsaken by men, a
Man of sorrows and pains, and
acquainted with grief and sickness;
and like one from whom men hide
their faces He was despised, and we
did not appreciate His worth or have
any esteem for Him. Surely He has
borne our grief's (sicknesses,
weaknesses, and distresses) and
carried our sorrows and pains [of

punishment], yet we [ignorantly] considered Him stricken, smitten, and afflicted by God [as if with leprosy]. But He was wounded for our transgressions, He was bruised for our guilt and iniquities; the chastisement [needful to obtain] peace and well-being for us was upon Him, and with the stripes [that wounded] Him we are healed and made whole. All we like sheep have gone astray, we have turned everyone to his own way; and the Lord has made to light upon Him the guilt and iniquity of us all (Isaiah 53: 3-6)

LIFE IS A CHOICE

The idea of long living is not what God will force on anyone. God has enough power to force His Laws on humanity being the Owner of us all but He chose not to force His Laws on us. The time should come when God will wants us to be matured enough to make decisions that will bless us and brings glory to His Name by choosing His ways. God's ways are not grievous, His yokes are easy to bear, all it takes is for us to accept Jesus Christ as our Lord and Saviour and dwell on His Words through constant study. By allowing The Wisdom of God to dwell in us richly, and to allow the word of God to mould our characters to the glory of God's Name. That is the reason why Deuteronomy 30: 19-20 encourages us to choose life. Each time we choose to study and meditate the Word of God, what we are choosing and receiving is life and not death.

I call heaven and earth to witness
this day against you that I have set
before you life and death, the
blessings and the curses; therefore
choose life that you and your
descendants may live. And may love
the Lord your God, obey His voice,
and cling to Him. For He is your life
and the length of your days, that you
may dwell in the land which the Lord
swore to give to your fathers, to
Abraham, Isaac, and Jacob
(Deuteronomy 30: 19-20)

It is not possible to miss your direction if you constantly listen to what God will have to say to you, the Bible assures us that in God's presence is the fullness of joy (Psalm 16:11)

CHAPTER FIVE

FORGIVENESS IN CHRIST

[God] has not beheld iniquity in
Jacob [for he is forgiven], neither
has He seen
mischief or perverseness in Israel
[for the same reason]. The Lord their
God is with Israel, and the shout of
praise to their King is among the
people (Numbers 23:21)

God does not wants us to be sin conscious, God wants us well at all times. He wants us to think constantly about how good God is, not on the negative wrong reports around us. The Bible says if anything is of good reports, if it will bless us, if it will glorify God, we must dwell on it, meaning that we can think about such reports constantly by fixing our minds on them.

For the rest, brethren, whatever is
true, whatever is worthy of
reverence and is
honourable and seemly, whatever is

just, whatever is pure, whatever is
lovely and lovable, whatever is
kind and winsome and gracious, if
there is any virtue and excellence, if
there is anything worthy of praise,
think on and weigh and take account
of these things [fix your minds on
them] (Philippians 4:8)

In Christ, we have forgiveness from sin, from all the
sin of the past, present or future. Do not allow satan
to keep reminding you about what you didn't do
right when you were growing up. Every humanity
will have the season in their lives when they were
learning to grow, when they were learning to walk
according to God's will for them.

………..the former troubles are
forgotten and because they are
hidden from My eyes. For behold, I
create new heavens and a new
earth. And the former things shall
not be remembered or come into
mind. But be glad and rejoice forever
in that which I create; for behold, I
create Jerusalem to be a rejoicing
and her people a joy (Isaiah 65: 16-
18)

Therefore for us to enjoy life and to have life in abundance, we must let go of what went wrong in the past, we must be willing to receive forgiveness and to give forgiveness and learn to protect and preserve that which belongs to us. Our focus should be on now and the blessings God promises to bring to our lives, not on the past mistakes. A good driver who does not wants to get into accident will not put all his or her focus on the rear mirror but on where he or she is going. May The Lord grant us more and more grace to focus on Him and all the blessings He is bringing our ways in The Name of Jesus Christ.

Do not [earnestly] remember the former things; neither consider the things of old. Behold, I am doing a new thing! Now it springs forth; do you not perceive and know it and will you not give heed to it? I will even make a way in the wilderness and rivers in the desert (Isaiah 43: 18-19)

I, even I, am He Who blots out and cancels your transgressions, for My own sake, and I will not remember your sins (Isaiah 43: 25)

Forgiving Others

Not keeping grudges against anyone is the quickest way to receive healing and forgiveness from God. Readily forgiving other people of their trespasses to us is a good way to be healthy, wealthy and robust in Christ. We are to do good to those that despitefully uses us. We must be willing to say sorry to those that thinks that we have offended them without arguments and without defending our rights always, knowing that while we are still on this planet people may offend us and we may not get everything right always. We must not be too hard to get along with. If we lack the urge or compassion to forgive anyone, we should fast and pray and ask The Holy Spirit to heal us of any previous wounds and to re-mould us by giving us His character, by creating in us His good original purpose for our lives.

Watch the Companies You Keep

Who are your friends? Surrounding yourself more with people who love the Lord and His Laws, those who are able to teach you and guide you into all truth is a good way to be healthy and robust in Christ. I pray that The Lord God will grant us the grace to appreciate men and women He will bring our ways to bless us in The Name of Jesus Christ.

Prayer

My prayer is that God will give each and every one of us God ordained friends and associates who are equipped and empowered to make the good and God ordained purposes to become reality in our lives in Jesus Mighty Name.

CHAPTER SIX

THERE IS NO FEAR IN CHRIST

There is no fear in love [dread does not exist], but full-grown (complete, perfect) love turns fear out of doors and expels every trace of terror... (1 John 4:18a)

Where the Spirit of The Living God dwells (The Word of God), fears cannot rule there. The Word of God is capable of terminating anything satan may want to plant in anyone's life in the form of fears. I pray that The Lord God will grant us the grace to constantly dwell in His secret places where no power of evils can come in The Name of Jesus Christ (see Psalm 91). Anything that constantly makes you panic or that constantly reminds you how you are going to be punished is not of God. Where the Spirit of The Living God dwells, where the Words of God abounds, there is no fear. There is peace, joy healing, love, prosperities and freedom from the threats of satan where the Spirit of The Living God dwells.

Rule in the midst of your enemies (Psalm110:1), rule in the midst of anything that tries to terrifies you. Rule in the midst of any mistakes of the past whilst you are waiting for God to perfect that which concerns you in The Name of Jesus Christ.

> For God did not give us a spirit of timidity (of cowardice, of craven and cringing and fawning fear), but [He has given us a spirit] of power and of love and of calm and well-balanced mind and discipline and self-control. Do not blush or be ashamed then, to testify to and for our Lord………. (2 Timothy 1: 7-8a)

Our testimony (our conversations) should be based on the goodness of God, it must be based on The Word of God. We must train our minds to meditate the Word of God, this we must do regularly to bless ourselves and our family. We must acquaint ourselves with the Word of God until satan finds it difficult to come near our spirit, soul and body and every things that belongs to us. Our testimonies and conversations can be in the form of prayers and meditating the Word of God.

God's desire for His Children is that they will be bold and be courageous in all situations, not to be timid or fearful about anything. The only fear God commands in the Bible is that we should have a referential fear of Him and not to be timid about any situation.

Be strong, courageous, and firm;
fear not nor be in terror before them,
for it is the Lord your God Who goes
with you; He will not fail you or
forsake you (Deuteronomy 31:6)

We must have the total conviction that wherever we go, it is God who goes before us. It is God who comes behind us and His power surrounds us in all situations. We may be asking the reason why God mentioned the words "Fear Not" in the several passages of The Bible. God did so because He doesn't want His Children to be timid about anything. There is no situation that God cannot fix, no mountain is too big for Him to conquer, at the appropriate time God knows how to glorify Himself and He will glorify Himself in our lives in The Name of Jesus Christ.

Fear not [there is nothing to fear], for I am with you; do not look around you in terror and be dismayed, for I am your God. I will strengthen and harden you to difficulties, yes, I will help you; yes, and I will hold you up and retain you with My [victorious] right hand of rightness and justice (Isaiah 41:10)

Fret Not

Do not fret or have any anxiety about anything, but in every circumstance and in everything, by prayer and petition (definite requests), with thanksgiving, continue to make your wants known to God (Philippians 4:6)

Fret not yourself because of evildoers, neither be envious against those who work unrighteousness (that which is not upright or in right standing with God) (Psalm 37:1)

Casting down Imaginations

The Bible advices us to cast down every wrong imaginations and everything that tries to exalt itself above the knowledge and the blessings of the Lord in our lives.

Poverty and sickness is not of God, therefore, we must cast off the spirit of poverty, lack or sickness always in The Name of Jesus Christ.

Torment and fear is not from God, therefore, we cast off to the pit of no returns every spirit of fear and torments in The Name of Jesus Christ.

Ignorance is not from God, we cast off every spirit of ignorance in The Name of Jesus Christ.

The Bible advices that we should judge ourselves, to make sure that we accept the full blessings Christ died to paid for, therefore anything lower than the full blessings Christ paid for in our lives is cast off in The Name of Jesus Christ. Fear and torments are cast off, sickness and death are cast off, poverty and lack are cast off in The Name of Jesus Christ.

Do Not Be Anxious About Anything

Do not fret or have any anxiety
about anything, but in every
circumstance and in everything, by
prayer and petition (definite
requests), with thanksgiving,
continue to make your wants known
to God. (Philippians 4:6)

We thank God for the abilities He gave unto us to constantly study His Word, meditate on them and to pray about all situations.

Divine Restoration

Then the Lord your God will restore
your fortunes and have compassion
upon you and will gather you again
from all the nations where He has
scattered you (Deuteronomy 30:3)

God promised to restore back to all His Children what satan stole from each and every one of us. God is not a liar, if anyone has lost anything precious to them. I will advise them to have their trust in The Living Word of God and to be expecting better returns from The Father God for all that satan has stolen from them. For every good things satan has stolen from us, God's Word advised that we should be expecting double recompense of every good things lost in The Name of Jesus Christ.

Instead of your [former] shame you shall have a twofold recompense; instead of dishonour and reproach [your people] shall rejoice in their portion. Therefore in their land they shall possess double [what they had forfeited]; everlasting joy shall be theirs (Isaiah 61:7)

For I the Lord love justice; I hate robbery and wrong with violence or a burnt offering. And I will faithfully give them their recompense in truth, and I will make an everlasting covenant or league with them. And their offspring shall be known among the nations and their descendants among the peoples. All who see them [in their prosperity] will

recognize and acknowledge that
they are the people whom the Lord
has blessed (Isaiah 61: 8-9)

Thinking about the promises of God to restored back unto us all that satan stole from us. We should be glad, celebrate and give praises unto The Lord always. Knowing that, for God to have promised the double restoration of all that satan stole from us, God will definitely bring to pass His promises.

Isaiah 61: 8-9 is our portion, it is our inheritance and we received it in The Name of Jesus Christ. Double blessings for all that satan stole from us in The Name of Jesus Christ. Our face shall no longer be sad and shameful in The Name of Jesus Christ.

CHAPTER SEVEN

ARISE AND SHINE FOR GOD

Arise [from the depression and
prostration in which circumstances
have kept you—rise to a new life]!
Shine (be radiant with the glory of
the Lord), for your light has come,
and the glory of the Lord has risen
upon you! (Isaiah 60:1)

Christian faith is not the faith for the poor people
only, it is not the faith where people are passive
waiting to go to heaven. It is not a faith that
encourages people to live in defeat, poverty,
regrets, lacks and penury. It is the faith that
empowers and energises people for every good
works. If you have accepted Jesus Christ as your
Lord and Saviour, the realm you should be living in
should be heavenly realms already, where there is
no scarcity of any good things. Where you should
eat your bread without sorrow. Where no evil can
come near you and your dwelling places. Where
only the voice of rejoicing and celebrations is the
daily happenings in your habitations. Where you

wear clean clothes, live in a clean house, drink clean waters and eat healthy diet.

Christ is not poor, God's intention for His Children is for them to enjoy life and have life in abundance (see John 10: 10b), not to just keep occupying spaces and barely surviving on meagre income. That is not the attributes of God the Owner of the planet earth, and that is not the attributes of God who created the world. My Father God is the Owner of the world, I cannot be living in abject poverty. God did not saved us so as to punish us (He did not saved us for punishment). He promised not to leave us as orphans.

I will not leave you as orphans
[comfortless, desolate, bereaved,
forlorn, helpless]; I will come [back]
to you (John 14: 18)

Therefore I advised someone to cast away the filthy rag that situations is trying to put on them, to return to The Word of God, to start putting their faith in Christ again. To be ready to accept their positions of authority to rule with their King again, for everything will work together for their good in The Name of Jesus Christ.

Casting Away the Garments of Widowhood

> But he who is the high priest among his brethren, upon whose head the anointing oil was poured and who is consecrated to put on the [sacred] **garments**, shall not let the hair of his head hang loose or rend his clothes [in mourning], (Leviticus 21: 9-11)

People may mourn after losing the member of their family or anything precious to them, but they must not mourn forever.

As the born again children of God, we shall not have any reason to mourn at all in The Name of Jesus Christ. Jesus Christ has conquered death for us, He defeated death for our sake several years ago, and therefore, we are alive and well in Christ. We have passed from death to life. The Holy Anointing oil has touched us at a time in life, therefore, we are anointed, the Bible advices that for everyone upon whose head the anointing oil was poured should not rend their clothes in mourning. In The Name of Jesus Christ, we shall not have

83

reasons to mourn at all in The Name of Jesus Christ. We are more than conquerors in The Name of Jesus Christ.

We must be willing to arise from the state of penury that circumstances may want to put us, we must shake off every wrong spirits that tries to attach itself to us. We must receive our healing and strength as quickly as possible. We must all be willing to cast away every garments of widowhood, and start wearing the Royal Robes The Father God will provide for us in The Name of Jesus Christ.

Healing starts from the mind, to be able to truly manifest the beauty of the Lord, to be truly radiate His glory, it must starts from inside out, and how to achieve this is by allowing the Word of God to dwell in us richly. The Word of God is capable of healing anyone, it is capable of making anyone to be sound in mind, and it is capable of making anyone to manifest the beauty of Our Lord and Saviour. As the elect and the ambassadors of God the Almighty, we should manifest cleanness in our appearances. It is not about wearing an expensive apparel, but it is in keeping the ones we have clean always. It is about being willing to keep ourselves and our environment clean always to the glory of Father, Son and The Holy Spirit. Our acts of goodness is capable of terminating the spirits of death, sadness, grief or depressions from our environment. Thereby making us to enjoy life in abundant.

Be Free From the Burial Wrappings

Culture, the traditions of men, situations and circumstances may want to deposit into your life the garments of mourning, they may wish you to be sorry for yourself for the rest of your life. You are the one who will make up your mind to cast away every wrong garments, wrong associations and every wrong spirits from your life in The Name of Jesus Christ.

Whatever the challenge you may have experienced in the past, whatever you may be going through, it shall not lead into your death in The Name of Jesus Christ if you have truly accepted Jesus Christ as your Lord and Saviour. You shall not walk into the wrong paths in The Name of Jesus Christ. In the Bible times, Jesus Christ was informed about the illness of His friend named Lazarus. The normal thing to do is for people to start panicking and weeping when informed about the loss of a relative or friend, but Jesus gave us some example that being calm in the face of certain situations will leads to some good results. Jesus was calmed when He received the news, and He prophesied by declaring the result He will accepted:

> When Jesus received the message,
> He said, This sickness is not to end

in death; but [on the contrary] it is to honour God and to promote His glory, that the Son of God may be glorified through (by) it (John 11:4)

Jesus Christ was saying in the face of the challenge that the situation will not result into death, that He will not accept death as the final results. Someone may say, shouldn't Jesus Christ have a humble spirit and flows with the majority? When it comes to faith, we do not declare what the majority declares, we only declares the counsels of God The Almighty.

I pray that The Lord God will empowers us to have the God kind of faith that will not settle for anything contrary to The Blessings of The Lord. We are not to go into agreement with anyone or any institutions against ourselves.

If you are the only one who will declare good things concerning you and your family, do so without feeling guilty. The only person you need to please is God and not any other arms of flesh.

Another occasion when Jesus Christ refused to cooperate with peoples opinion concerning the death of someone was in the case of Jairus daughter in Luke 8; 49-50

While He was still speaking, a man from the house of the director of the synagogue came and said [to Jairus], Your daughter is dead; do not weary and trouble the Teacher any further. But Jesus, on hearing this, answered him, Do not be seized with alarm or struck with fear; simply believe in Me as able to do this], and she shall be made well (Luke 8: 49-50)

Jesus will never cooperate with any spirit regarding the death of anyone even before and after His crucifixion. Jesus Christ will always declare His expectations concerning a situation, not what someone wants Him to accept.

It is a shame for anyone not to accept the death of Jesus Christ as the final price for all humanity. It is a shame and an act of ignorance to allow satan to sow the wrong thoughts of death into our spirit. The day we accept Jesus Christ as our Lord and Saviour was the day we moved from death to live. Before we accepted Jesus Christ as our Lord and Saviour, we were living a sinful, ignorant lifestyle, depending on our own abilities, thinking and imaginations, but since when we become born again, Christ came into our lives, He took our sinful nature and gave us His righteousness, He gave us life immortal, He justify us fully.

This sickness is not to end in death, that pain is not to end in death, the symptoms is not to end in death, stop thinking about death and start focusing on the glorious and beautiful future God has for you. God still works miracles.

Rise to a New Life

Isaiah 60:1 advices us to arise from any forms of depression we may have found ourselves. To be willing to let go of the past by not focusing too much on them, to be prepared and be willing to receive the new blessings God is about to bring into our lives.

Do not [earnestly] remember the former things; neither consider the things of old. Behold, I am doing a new thing! Now it springs forth; do you not perceive and know it and will you not give heed to it? I will even make a way in the wilderness and rivers in the desert. (Isaiah 43: 18-19)

The Bible has been written for us as an example for us to follow, Jesus Christ prophesied it that if we only believe in Him, greater works of miracles we shall all do in The Name of Jesus Christ.

I assure you, most solemnly I tell you, if anyone steadfastly believes in Me, he will himself be able to do the things that I do; and he will do even greater things than these (John 14: 12)

Pray for One Another That You May be Healed

....pray [also] for one another, that you may be healed and restored [to a spiritual tone of mind and heart]. The earnest (heartfelt, continued) prayer of a righteous man makes tremendous power available [dynamic in its working] (James 5: 16)

The scriptures cannot be broken, the Word of God is settled forever. We were advised by The Word of God to pray and not to faint and to pray always (Luke 18:1). The prayers that is of faith makes tremendous power available.

Fresh Oil

Father God we receive the wisdom, courage and empowerments to pray always without ceasing, to remember to pray for someone, knowing that in their well beings is our own wellbeing. Knowing that if it is well with our neighbours and family, that is a gain for us. It is to our own advantage if it is well with our neighbours and friends. It is to our own advantage when our family and friends act according to the will and the blessings of The Lord. It is to our own advantage when our governments makes laws that will blesses us and not harms us. Wishing someone well and praying for them will lead to our own healing and restored joy unto us in The Name of Jesus Christ. It is a bonus for us if someone that supposed to help us is well, therefore we don't wait till when someone will be sick before we start declaring and prophesying good things concerning them in The Name of Jesus Christ.

If you have been trained to always wait for someone to pray for you, it is about the time when you should be ready to start praying for someone. Praying for someone is not for you to go and starts looking for someone to lay your hands on, you can pray for someone from distance and God will answers your prayers. Not all prayers needs to be loud, not everyone you pray for needs to know that you are praying for them (see the prayer of Hannah in 1 Samuel 1: 12-13) your rewards come from above (from The Father who shows no partiality, from God The Father who sent you) The Father who sees in the secret, He will rewards you in the open. I pray that God will continue to empower us to do things according to His ways.

Your prayer for someone is capable of making you well, it can give you a good conscience, and it can save you from blood guiltiness. If your family and friends are well, it will boost your own wellbeing.

See 1 Timothy 2: 1-4 and 1 Samuel 1:10-14

The man in John 11 (Lazarus) eventually died and Bible recorded that his body was stinking by the time Jesus arrived at the destination, but Jesus shouted with a loud voice "Lazarus come out" and the man rose from the dead, walking with his hands and feet's wrapped in burial cloths, and Jesus said to the people around him "free him of the burial wrappings.

Jesus said to them, Free him of the
burial wrappings and let him go
(John 11:44)

91

I pray that every traces of the burial wrappings and the deadly situations around anyone be removed in The Name of Jesus Christ.

Today I cast away from my life every burial wrappings. I cast away from my life every burial conditions. Today is the day that every spirit of death dies in my life beyond resurrections in The Name of Jesus Christ.

The Story of The Resurrection power of God started in The Garden of Eden when satan crawled into the lives of Adam and Eve with the intention of causing death, but instantly God came into the situation and cast away satans intentions. God rebuked satan for their sakes, and He cursed satan for their sakes, and God gave Adam and Eve His covenant and promises of Salvation. God has been in the business of saving souls right from the beginning.

If we look a bit further into the first few chapters of the Bible, God promised that He will not forever strife with man, for he is a flesh and He even gave them a covenant of Long Living, not a short one.

GIVE YOUR EARS TO GODS WORD AND NOT TO THE TRADITIONS OF MEN

DO NOT BE AFRAID OF THEIR FACES

WHAT IS MAN THAT YOU ARE MINDFUL OF HIM

KNOWING WHAT YOU HAVE IN CHRIST (Eternal Life)

> I assure you, most solemnly I tell
> you, he who believes in Me [who
> adheres to, trusts in, relies on, and
> has faith in Me] has (now
> possesses) eternal life (John 6: 47)

There is no Death in Christ

If you are a Christian, I mean a born again child of God, you have to be clear about what the Lord did for you the day you accepted Christ as your Lord and Saviour; it was that you passed from death to life, therefore we say, there is no death in Christ.

> I assure you, most solemnly I tell
> you, the person whose ears are
> open to My words [who listens to My
> message] and believes and trusts in
> and clings to and relies on Him Who
> sent Me has (possesses now)

eternal life. And he does not come
into judgment [does not incur
sentence of judgment, will not come
under condemnation], but he has
already passed over out of death
into life. Believe Me when I assure
you, most solemnly I tell you, the
time is coming and is here now
when the dead shall hear the voice
of the Son of God and those who
hear it shall live (John 5: 24-25).

And those who hear the Word of God shall live and
not die, the Word of God only leads to life,
longevity, healing, strength and prosperities, any
word that does not give you life more abundantly is
of the devil, try and avoid them.

Because he has set his love upon
Me, therefore will I deliver him; I will
set him on high, because he
knows and understands My name
[has a personal knowledge of My
mercy, love, and kindness—trusts
and relies on Me, knowing I will
never forsake him, no, never]. He
shall call upon Me, and I will answer
him; I will be with him in trouble, I will

94

deliver him and honour him. With long life will I satisfy him and show him My salvation. (Psalm 91:14-16)

But be glad and rejoice forever in that which I create; for behold, I create Jerusalem to be a rejoicing and her people a joy. And I will rejoice in Jerusalem and be glad in My people; and the sound of weeping will no more be heard in it, nor the cry of distress. There shall no more be in it an infant who lives but a few days, or an old man who dies prematurely; for the child shall die a hundred years old, and the sinner who dies when only a hundred years old shall be [thought only a child, cut off because he is] accursed. They shall build houses and inhabit them, and they shall plant vineyards and eat the fruit of them. They shall not build and another inhabit; they shall not plant and another eat [the fruit]. For as the days of a tree, so shall be the days of My people, and My chosen and elect shall long make use of and enjoy the work of their hands. They shall not labour in vain or bring forth [children] for sudden terror or calamity; for they shall be the descendants of the blessed of the Lord, and their offspring with them. And it shall be that before they call I will answer; and while they are yet speaking I will hear (Isaiah 65: 18-24)

Then the Lord said, My Spirit shall not forever dwell and strive with man, for he also is flesh; but his days shall yet be 120 years. (Genesis 6:3)

But if you are guided (led) by the [Holy] Spirit, you are not subject to the Law. (Galatians 5:18)

See also: Galatians 5:19-26

Choose to Be Well: Your Life May Be The Mirror of God to Someone.

You may be the perfect encourager God will use to encourage someone to launch them into their destiny. Choose to be well and strong, choose to prosper in Christ. Let people see the beauty of Christ through you. Be determined that you will make it in life beyond the winning line. Be determined to be full of good deeds to the glory of God.

God encouraged the Children of Israel while they were in the wilderness, on their way to The Promised Land. God gave them the code of conducts for a good, healthy living lifestyle, so that they can have enough strength to make it through to The Promised Land.

Do not give room for anything that will not make you to manifest the best for God. Your generation is waiting for you, you may be the only role model God will use to launch someone into His blessings for them, present yourself in a way that honours God. The Bible says the whole creation is waiting for the manifestations of the sons of God.

For [even the whole] creation (all nature) waits expectantly and longs earnestly for God's sons to be made known [waits for the revealing, the disclosing of their sonship] (Romans 8: 19)

Make your arrival to be beautiful, make it glorious, and give Nations the opportunity to thank God for His faithfulness to you.

How Can We Achieve This

Just as we have discussed, The Word of God must enter through our eyes and ears regularly. The Spirit of The Living God must dwell in us richly. We must allow the Word of God to flush away from us every wrong teachings and imaginations.

I pray that the Scriptures shall be fulfilled in the lives of each and every one of us in The Name of Jesus Christ. That nothing will be able to separate us from the love of God which is in Christ Jesus.

Yet amid all these things we are more than conquerors and gain a surpassing victory through Him Who loved us. For I am persuaded beyond doubt (am sure) that neither death nor life, nor angels nor principalities, nor things

98

impending and threatening nor
things to come, nor powers, nor
height nor depth, nor anything else
in all creation will be able to
separate us from the love of God
which is in Christ Jesus our Lord
(Romans 8: 37-39)

CHAPTER EIGHT

RESTORATIONS FROM DEATH

Jesus replied to them, Go and report
to John what you hear and see. The
blind receive their sight and the lame
walk, lepers are cleansed (by
healing) and the deaf hear, the dead
are raised up and the poor have
good news (the Gospel) preached to
them (Matthew 11: 4-5)

Most of us have had the experiences of the
faithfulness of God to His Words concerning our
salvation. On a daily basis God saved His own from
known and unknown near death experiences and
situations. We sleep and wake up, only God
sustains us. Travelling from one destination to
others, only God keeps us from all forms of
dangers. Some have been through some situations
that almost kill them, but by the grace of God they
came out with no injury. Most human being can
testify to some situations they know it must have

been God who saved them and not of their own making.

In the Bible time especially in the books of The New Testament, there are records of where Jesus brought back to life souls that satan tried to terminate prematurely. Jesus Christ arose from the grave after three days, conquering death, bringing victory over death to humanity and freeing humanity from the fear of death. And Jesus Christ gave everyone who believes in Him the power to do even greater works than He does by transferring the power unto us.

Cure the Sick and Raise the Dead

But go rather to the lost sheep of the house of Israel. And as you go, preach, saying, the kingdom of heaven is at hand! Cure the sick, raise the dead, cleanse the lepers, and drive out demons. Freely (without pay) you have received, freely (without charge) give (Matthew 10: 6-8)

The Father God has empowered humanity with much power to work wonders on His behalf. We have to be very careful that we do not throw away our covenant rights through ignorance. We thank God for all the miracles we see in our midst today. I believe most of the miracles have been made possible only by The Power of The Holy Ghost, by God empowering His people to do good. The miracles we see through our medical science and our churches has been made possible by God. We should know that God doesn't wants all our total dependency to be on the medical science. God will train and teach us to learn to endure, especially for the days when we may not have quick access to the medical helps. If we have been trained to know that our life is not in the hand of medical science, the death rate in our society shall be reduced in The Name of Jesus Christ. We shall not be losing those who are meant to build our society to death.

There is a volume of pressure we can placed on our medical science, the people that operate most of the medical science equipment's are human. It will be a good idea to give our medical department the time to attend to only the very urgent and important matters simply because we have successfully raised healthy generations. If we choose to be well and healthy, we would have time to attend to other important matters in our land, we would be able to work to provide for all our basic amenities. No good leaders will wants to see most of their populations to be on sick bed, nor parents who should take good care of their children to be sick always. We must pray and promote ways for our citizens to be well, no nation can provide enough medical bed to accommodate patient without the help of God. For everyone that prays against premature death in our midst, their generations shall not be wiped out from the planet earth and from the world in The Name of Jesus Christ. Those who have not been praying, may God empowers them to start doing so in The Name of Jesus Christ.

For everyone that supports the cause of Christ, heaven shall defends them too in The Name of Jesus Christ. God will terminate every programs that have caused unnecessary death in our land. God will terminate every wrong programs and counsels in The Name of Jesus Christ. The voice of the righteous shall be heard in our lands in The Name of Jesus Christ.

The Lord God shall terminate every wrong teachings in The Name of Jesus Christ. The Lord God will empowers the righteous to be bold to stand to defend the just causes in The Name of Jesus Christ.

In the Bible time and till today, the miracles of healing and raising the dead back to life has never ceased in our midst and it shall continue in The

Name of Jesus Christ. I love the reply Jesus sent to John the Baptist in the book of Matthew 11: 4-5)

> And Jesus replied to them, Go and
> report to John what you hear and
> see. The blind receive their sight and
> the lame walk, lepers are cleansed
> (by healing) and the deaf hear, the
> dead are raised up and the poor
> have good news (the Gospel)
> preached to them (Matthew 11: 4-5)

In the book of Matthew chapter 10 Jesus commissioned His disciples to go and heal the sick and raise the dead. If God has given anyone an assignment, He shall back them up. In the book of Acts, there are records of the Disciples performing series of miracles including raising the dead. One of the awesome miracles performed by one of the disciples named Peter was healing the man that has been bedfast for eight years. Also one of the disciples by the name Dorcas (Tabitha) was also raised back to life from dead. I have a good news for someone, God still works miracles, and your days of weeping is over in The Name of Jesus Christ. Your good testimony shall be a wonder to the world, your good testimony shall make nations to turn to The Word of God in The Name of Jesus

Christ. What satan has stolen from you shall be returned unto you in million folds in The Name of Jesus Christ.

Greater Works than These You Shall Do

Greater works that these you shall do is the Word of Jesus Christ to His disciples. Each and every one of us, as the believers and the disciples of Jesus Christ has been commissioned to go and do greater works for our own benefits and enjoyments, to bless someone and to bring glory to The Name of Jesus Christ. I pray that no one or any forces will be big enough to stop The Word of God from becoming a good reality in our lives in The Name of Jesus Christ. I pray the Wisdom of God will dwell in each and every one of us abundantly to prepare us for the Greater Tasks God has for us in The Name of Jesus Christ. I pray that The Word of God will prosper us and bless each and every one of us abundantly in The Name of Jesus Christ.

I assure you, most solemnly I tell you, if anyone steadfastly believes in Me, he will himself be able to do the things that I do; and he will do even greater things than these (John 14:12)

The Story of Aeneas

Now as Peter went here and there among them all, he went down also to the saints who lived at Lydda. There he found a man named Aeneas, who had been bedfast for eight years and was paralyzed. And Peter said to him, Aeneas, Jesus Christ (the Messiah) [now] makes you whole. Get up and make your bed! And immediately [Aeneas] stood up. Then all the inhabitants of Lydda and the plain of Sharon saw [what had happened to] him and they turned to the Lord (Acts 9: 32-35)

The Story of Dorcas

Now there was at Joppa a disciple [a woman] named [in Aramaic] Tabitha, which [in Greek] means Dorcas. She was abounding in good deeds and acts of charity. About that time she fell sick and died, and when they had cleansed her, they laid [her] in an upper room. Since Lydda was near Joppa [however], the disciples, hearing that Peter was there, sent two men to him begging him, do come to us without delay. So Peter [immediately] rose and accompanied them. And when he had arrived, they took him to the upper room. All the widows stood around him, crying and displaying undershirts (tunics) and [other] garments such as Dorcas was accustomed to make while she was with them. But Peter put them all out [of the room] and knelt down and prayed; then turning to the body he said, Tabitha, get up! And she opened her eyes; and when she saw Peter, she raised herself and sat upright. And he gave her his hand and lifted her up. Then calling in God's people and the widows, he presented her to them alive. And this became known throughout all Joppa, and many came to believe on the Lord [to adhere to and trust in and rely on Him as the Christ and as their Saviour]. And Peter remained in Joppa for considerable time with a certain Simon a tanner (Acts 9: 36-43)

The story of Aeneas and Dorcas proved that God can works miracles through anyone. You have some good gifts and the power of the Holy Spirit within you that no one should underestimate. God shall works wonders through each and every one of us in The Name of Jesus Christ.

God Still Works Miracles

I am sure nobody is wondering whether God still works miracles today. Just in case there is a doubt in anyone, look at the miracles in the churches worldwide as at date, search churches through the internet and see the miracles of souls that God adds to the churches daily. The levels of the increase has been amazing, most churches can be reached through their website, see how God is adding to churches today souls that has been saved and that needs to be saved.

I am not talking about miracles among one tribe or one continent, miracles happens around the world on a daily basis especially in the life of those who are willing to humble themselves before God. God still works miracles.

Constantly praising God and being in favour and goodwill with all the people; and the Lord kept adding [to their number] daily those who were being saved [from spiritual death] (Acts 2:47)

CHAPTER NINE

HEALING

He who dwells in the secret place of
the Most High shall remain stable
and fixed under the shadow of the
Almighty [Whose power no foe can
withstand] (Psalm 91:1)

To be truly come out of every unpleasant situations,
we must not be too busy to feed our spirit, soul and
body with the Word of God. He who dwell in the
secret place of the most High shall be protected
from all kind of evils. The Lord God prepared the
Children of Israel and led them to the Promised
Land. On their way and throughout their journeys,
God guided them as to what they needs to do that
will make them to truly come out victoriously. He
wanted them to be in good health by the time they
reached the Promised Land; He doesn't want them
broken and battered.

The Word of God promised more blessings to those
whose minds stayed on Him (see Isaiah 26:3)

We must not love the world more than The Word of God, the measure we give to the Word of God will determine what we will get from God. I pray that The Lord God will grant us the grace to love and embrace His Words in The Name of Jesus Christ.

To enjoy the healing and health God planned for us to have, we must not be sin, sickness or poverty conscious, and we must be more of God's Word conscious. We must give more attention to the Word of God and be more healing conscious with The Word of God He gave us in The Bible dwelling in us richly.

God never asked us to be sickness symptoms conscious. He never asked us to be the medical science words conscious, God wants our attentions to be on His good promises for us. He wants us to be full of Him, not to be full of our symptoms, feelings, nor our challenges. He want us to start thinking and says what He says not what satan wants us to say and not what our symptoms tries to dictate to us.

Be More of God's Word conscious and not sickness conscious.

The word of God must dwell in us richly enough to flush away from us every wrong thinking's.

Resist the devil, it will flee from you is what the Bible says. We must not dwell on the symptoms of sickness, and we must not dwell on any wrong feelings, but rather to dwell on the Word of God, to meditate on the Word of God, to ponder over it. As we give more attentions to the Father God's Word as it is in the Bible, God will give us healing and not sickness.

God desired the Children of Israel to be well on their way to the Promised Land. He advised them on the types of foods they should eat and what they should not eat. He advised them to fast to discipline their flesh. He advised them to have control over their flesh and their eating habits (Leviticus 16:29, 1 Cor. 6:13)

> It shall be a statute to you forever that in the seventh month [nearly October] on the tenth day of the month you shall afflict yourselves [by fasting with penitence and humiliation] and do no work at all, either the native-born or the stranger who dwells temporarily among you. For on this day atonement shall be made for you, to cleanse you; from all your sins you shall be clean before the Lord. It is a Sabbath of [solemn] rest to you, and you shall

afflict yourselves [by fasting with
penitence and humiliation]; it is a
statute forever (Leviticus 16: 29-31)

Though God advised the Israelites to fast in the
tenth day of the seventh month, Christians should
fast and pray as God leads them always and God
will give a Sabbath of rest from any activities that is
not profitable to us. He will save us from every
activities that does not bring glory to The Name of
The Lord. He will prepared us and save us from
anything that is trying to distract us from enjoying
God's best for us. Therefore, it does not mean
being idle doing nothing, it means being able to
slow down to hear God's best directions for us. As
soon as we hear Him, we should follow the
directions. I pray that we will be able to hear God
and obey in The Name of Jesus Christ. I pray that
God will grant us the Wisdom, the Spirit of
understanding, the finances, the energy and the
time to study His Words.

Scriptures on Healing

Saying, If you will diligently hearken to the voice of
the Lord your God and will do what is right in His
sight, and will listen to and obey His
commandments and keep all His statutes, I will put
none of the diseases upon you which I brought

upon the Egyptians, for I am the Lord Who heals you (Exodus 15:26)

Bless (affectionately, gratefully praise) the Lord, O my soul; and all that is [deepest] within me, bless His holy name! Bless (affectionately, gratefully praise) the Lord, O my soul, and forget not [one of] all His benefits— Who forgives [every one of] all your iniquities, Who heals [each one of] all your diseases. Who redeems your life from the pit and corruption, Who beautifies, dignifies, and crowns you with loving-kindness and tender mercy. Who satisfies your mouth [your necessity and desire at your personal age and situation] with good so that your youth, renewed, is like the eagle's [strong, overcoming, soaring]! (Psalm 103: 1-5)

Surely He has borne our grief's (sicknesses, weaknesses, and distresses) and carried our sorrows and pains [of punishment], yet we [ignorantly] considered Him stricken, smitten, and afflicted by God [as if with leprosy]. But He was wounded for our transgressions, He was bruised for our guilt and iniquities; the chastisement [needful to obtain] peace and well-being for us was upon Him, and with the stripes [that wounded] Him we are healed and made whole (Isaiah 53: 4-5)

So the report of Him spread throughout all Syria, and they brought Him all who were sick, those afflicted with various diseases and torments, those under the power of demons, and epileptics, and paralyzed people, and He healed them (Matthew 4:24)

When evening came, they brought to Him many who were under the power of demons, and He drove out the spirits with a word and restored to health all who were sick. And thus He fulfilled what was spoken by the prophet Isaiah, He Himself took [in order to carry away] our weaknesses and infirmities and bore away our diseases (Matthew 8: 16-17)

Jesus turned around and, seeing her, He said, Take courage, daughter! Your faith has made you well. And at once the woman was restored to health (Matthew 9:22)

And Jesus, in pity, touched their eyes; and instantly they received their sight and followed Him (Matthew 20:34)

And the blind and the lame came to Him in the porches and courts of the temple, and He cured them (Matthew 21:14)

For He had healed so many that all who had distressing bodily diseases kept falling upon Him and pressing upon Him in order that they might touch Him (Mark 3: 10)

For Jesus was commanding, Come out of the man, you unclean spirit! (Mark 5:8)

And they came to Jesus and looked intently and searchingly at the man who had been a demoniac, sitting there, clothed and in his right mind, [the same man] who had had the legion [of demons]; and they were seized with alarm and struck with fear (Mark 5:15)

And He said to her, Daughter, your faith (your trust and confidence in Me, springing from faith in God) has restored you to health. Go in (into) peace and be continually healed and freed from your [distressing bodily] disease (Mark 5:34)

And when He had gone in, He said to them, why do you make an uproar and weep? The little girl is not dead but is sleeping (Mark 5:39)

Gripping her [firmly] by the hand, He said to her, Talitha cumi—which translated is, little girl, I say to you, arise [from the sleep of death]! And instantly the girl got up and started walking around—for she was twelve years old. And they were utterly astonished and overcome with amazement. And He strictly commanded and warned them that no one should know this, and He [expressly] told them to give her [something] to eat (Mark 5: 41-43)

And He called to Him the Twelve [apostles] and began to send them out [as His ambassadors] two by two and gave them authority and power over the unclean spirits (Mark 6:7)

And wherever He came into villages or cities or the country, they would lay the sick in the marketplaces and beg Him that they might touch even the fringe of His outer garment, **and as many as touched Him were restored to health** (Mark 6: 56)

And He said to her, Because of this saying, you may go your way; the demon has gone out of your daughter [permanently]. And she went home and found the child thrown on the couch, and the demon departed (Mark 7: 29-30)

And they were overwhelmingly astonished, saying, He has done everything excellently (commendably and nobly)! He even makes the deaf to hear and the dumb to speak!
(Mark 7:37)

And God did unusual and extraordinary miracles by the hands of Paul. So that handkerchiefs or towels or aprons which had touched his skin were carried away and put upon the sick, and their diseases left them and the evil spirits came out of them (Acts 19: 11-12)

In conclusion, be strong in the Lord [**be empowered through your union with Him**]; draw your strength from Him [that strength which His boundless might provides]. Put on God's whole armour [the armour of a heavy-armed soldier which God supplies], that you may be able successfully to stand up against [all] the strategies and the deceits of the devil. For we are not wrestling with flesh and blood [contending only with physical opponents], but against the despotisms, against the powers, against [the master spirits who are] the world rulers of this present darkness, against the spirit forces of wickedness in the heavenly (supernatural) sphere (Ephesians 6:10-12)

For this is the covenant that I will make with the house of Israel after those days, says the Lord: I will imprint My laws upon their minds, even upon their innermost thoughts and understanding, and engrave them upon their hearts; and I will be their God, and they shall be My people (Hebrews 8:10)

He personally bore our sins in His [own] body on the tree [as on an altar and offered
Himself on it], that we might die (cease to exist) to sin and live to righteousness. By His wounds you have been healed (1 Peter 2:24)

CHAPTER TEN

PROSPERITY

Beloved, I pray that you may prosper
in every way and [that your body]
may keep well, even as [I know] your
soul keeps well and prospers (3
John 1:2)

Our prosperities pleases God, every Christian must be willing to fight to remove the wrong spirit of poverty from their lives. The price Jesus paid is not for us to be existing and start waiting to go to heaven only, but to enjoy prosperities while still on this planet. God delights in our prosperities, it pleases God when we have all our needs meet and have surplus remaining to give towards all charitable works.

Christian faith is not just to save you and then abandon you in regrets the remaining of your days. As we continue to choose to be well, as our souls continue to prosper, as we continue to give praises unto God, we must be willing to come out of poverty that has us bound unnecessarily. Having our needs meet in abundant is part of the longevity God promises us.

> God brought them forth out of Egypt;
> they have as it were the strength of
> a wild ox.

> Surely there is no enchantment
> with or against Jacob, neither is
> there any divination with or against
> Israel. [In due season and even] now
> it shall be said of Jacob and of
> Israel, What has God wrought!

(Numbers 23: 22-23)

Our prosperities pleases God, God wants us to enjoy life, to have life and enjoy it in abundance. That is one of the reason why Jesus came to save us. He did not save us to leave us in abject poverty. If anyone is not living above the standard blessings set by God The Almighty, then they should pray and ask God to empower them to start doing so.

For us to be truly prosperous, our souls must prospers in The Word of God. We must make the sacrifice of setting time apart to study the Word of God concerning all things, especially on how to manage our resources well. To be truly prosperous, we must prosper in all things. We must prosper in our relationship with God and with man. If we lack what it takes to build a good God glorifying relationships that endure (last) we should pray to God to empower us with the ability to do so.

Choosing to study The Word of God on all subjects and topics is the quickest route to learn the will of God and form the habit of obeying them. From Genesis to Revelations, God emphasises that He delights in the prosperity of His Children. Gods Promises to bless us is certain: Gods prosperity plans for us is certain. God's plan to bless us is certain, they are yes and amen. God promises to remove every spirit of wretchedness from His people.

And He will destroy on this mountain
the covering of the face that is cast
over the heads of all peoples [in
mourning], and the veil [of profound
wretchedness] that is
woven and spread over all nations.
He will swallow up death [in victory;
He will abolish death forever]. And
the Lord God will wipe away tears
from all faces; and the reproach of
His people He will take away from off
all the earth; for the Lord has spoken
it (Isaiah 25: 7-8)

Christic is Not Poor

> And as He was praying, the appearance of His countenance became altered (different), and His raiment became dazzling white [flashing with the brilliance of lightning]. And behold, two men were conversing with Him—Moses and Elijah,
>
> **Who appeared in splendour and majesty and brightness ....
> (Luke 9: 29-31)**

Splendour, Majesty and Brightness is not a sign of poverty, but a sign of wealth. God wants His Children to manifest His Blessings and wealth everywhere they go. He wants the world to see that we are truly blessed and not curse. I pray that all our actions will lead us to manifest God's Blessings and not poverty and lack in The Name of Jesus Christ.

Think Big. It Pleases God

> And they saw the God of Israel [that is, a convincing manifestation of His presence], and under His feet it was

like pavement of bright sapphire
stone, like the very heavens in
clearness. And upon the nobles of
the Israelites He laid not His hand [to
conceal Himself from them, to
rebuke their daring, or to harm
them]; but they saw [the
manifestation of the presence of]
God, and ate and drank (Exodus
24:10-11)

In your attempt to come out of bondage, men may
try to rebuke you, but God will not rebuke you. The
brother of David tried to rebuke him for his daring to
come forward to fight the Goliath, to attempt
something great for God but God gave him the
grace to withstand them, God gave him the grace to
ignore them (1 Samuel 17: 26-37) The Bible
advices that we should not be afraid of their faces:

Before I formed you in the womb I
knew [and] approved of you [as My
chosen instrument], and before you
were born I separated and set you
apart, consecrating you; [and] I
appointed you as a prophet to the
nations. Then said I, Ah, Lord God!
Behold, I cannot speak, for I am only
a youth. But the Lord said to me,

127

Say not, I am only a youth; for you
shall go to all to whom I shall send
you, and whatever I command you,
you shall speak. Be not afraid of
them [their faces], for I am with you
to deliver you, says the Lord
(Jeremiah 1: 5-8)

Victory in Christ Jesus

No weapon formed against you to stop you from
rising, to stop you from achieving your God's given
purpose shall prosper in The Name of Jesus Christ.
If anyone or anything tries to rebuke you while you
are trying to achieve your God's given purpose, the
rebuke shall not prosper in The Name of Jesus
Christ.

Scriptures That Reminds Us That
God Delights in Our Prosperity

Then the Lord said to Moses, Behold, I will rain
bread from the heavens for you; and the people
shall go out and gather a day's portion every
day. That I may prove them, whether they will
walk in My law or not (Exodus 16:4)

So Moses and Aaron said to all Israel, at evening **you shall know** that the Lord has brought you out from the land of Egypt (Exodus 16:6)

And when the dew had gone, behold, upon the face of the wilderness there lay a fine, round and flakelike thing, as fine as hoarfrost on the ground (Exodus 16:14)

And Moses said, this is the thing which the Lord commanded you to do, and the glory of the Lord will appear to you……. Moses and Aaron went into the Tent of Meeting, and when they came out they blessed the people, and the glory of the Lord [the Shekinah cloud] appeared to all the people [as promised] (Leviticus 9:6, 23)

But you shall [earnestly] remember the Lord your God, for it is He Who gives you power to get wealth, that He may establish His covenant which He swore to your fathers, as it is this day (Deuteronomy 8:18)

For the land which you go in to possess is not like the land of Egypt, from which you came out, where you sowed your seed and watered it with your foot laboriously as in a garden of vegetables. But the land which you enter to possess is a land of hills and valleys which drinks water of the rain of the heavens. A land for which the Lord your God cares; the eyes of the Lord your God are always upon it from the beginning of the year to the end of the year. And if you will diligently heed My commandments which I command you this day—to love the Lord your God and to serve Him with all your [mind and] heart and with your entire being— I will give the rain for your land in its season, the early rain and the latter rain, that you may gather in your grain, your new wine, and your oil. And I will give grass in your fields for your cattle that you may eat and be full. (Deuteronomy 11:10-15)

God is not a man that He should tell or act a lie, neither the son of man, that He should feel repentance or compunction [for what He has promised]. Has He said and shall He not do it? Or has He spoken and shall He not make it good? You see, I have received His command to bless Israel. He has blessed, and I cannot reverse or qualify it. (Numbers 23: 19-20)

If you will listen diligently to the voice of the Lord your God, being watchful to do all His commandments which I command you this day, the Lord your God will set you high above all the nations of the earth. And all these blessings shall come upon you and overtake you if you heed the voice of the Lord your God. Blessed shall you be in the city and blessed shall you be in the field. Blessed shall be the fruit of your body and the fruit of your ground and the fruit of your beasts, the increase of your cattle and the young of your flock. Blessed shall be your basket and your kneading trough. Blessed shall you be when you come in and blessed shall you be when you go out. The Lord shall cause your enemies who rise up against you to be defeated before your face; they shall come out against you one way and flee before you seven ways. The Lord shall command the blessing upon you in your storehouse and in all that you undertake. And He will bless you in the land which the Lord your God gives you. The Lord will establish you as a people holy to Himself, as He has sworn to you, if you keep the commandments of the Lord your God and walk in His ways. And all people of the earth shall see that you are called by the name [and in the presence of] the Lord, and they shall be afraid of you. And the Lord shall make you have a surplus of prosperity, through the fruit of your body, of your livestock, and of your ground, in the land which the Lord swore to your fathers to give you. The Lord shall open to you His good treasury, the heavens, to give the rain of your land in its season and to bless all the work of your hands; and you shall lend to many nations, but you shall not borrow. And the

Lord shall make you the head, and not the tail; and you shall be above only, and you shall not be beneath, if you heed the commandments of the Lord your God which I command you this day and are watchful to do them. And you shall not turn aside from any of the words which I command you this day, to the right hand or to the left, to go after other gods to serve them. (Deuteronomy 28:1-14)

God is not a man that He should tell or act a lie, neither the son of man, that He should feel repentance or compunction [for what He has promised]. Has He said and shall He not do it? Or has He spoken and shall He not make it good? You see, I have received His command to bless Israel. He has blessed, and I cannot reverse or qualify it. **[God] has not beheld iniquity in Jacob [for he is forgiven],** neither has He seen mischief or perverseness in Israel [for the same reason]. The Lord their God is with Israel, and the shout of praise to their King is among the people. God brought them forth out of Egypt; they have as it were the strength of a wild ox. Surely there is no enchantment with or against Jacob, neither is there any divination with or against Israel. [In due season and even] now it shall be said of Jacob and of Israel, What has God wrought! (Numbers 23:19-23)

Hannah said, let your handmaid find grace in your sight. So [she] went her way and ate, **her countenance no longer sad.** The family rose early the next morning, worshiped before the Lord, and returned to their home in Ramah. Elkanah knew Hannah his wife, and the Lord remembered her (1 Samuel 1:18-19)

.........on the fourteenth day they rested and made it a day of feasting and gladness. But the Jews who were in Shushan [Susa] assembled on the thirteenth day and on the fourteenth, and on the fifteenth day they rested and made it a day of feasting and gladness. Therefore the Jews of the villages, who dwell in the unwalled towns, make the fourteenth day of the month of Adar a day of gladness and feasting, a holiday, and a day for sending choice portions to one another(Esther 9: 17-19)

Blessed (happy, fortunate, prosperous, and enviable) is the man who walks and lives not in the counsel of the ungodly [following their advice, their plans and purposes], nor stands [submissive and inactive] in the path where sinners walk, nor sits down [to relax and rest] where the scornful [and the mockers] gather. But his delight and desire are in the law of the Lord, and on His law (the precepts, the instructions, the teachings of God) he habitually meditates (ponders and studies) by day and by night. And he shall be like a tree firmly planted [and tended] by the streams of water, ready to bring forth its fruit in its season; its leaf also shall not fade or wither; and everything he does shall prosper [and come to maturity] (Psalms 1: 1-3)

Sing, O barren one, you who did not bear; break forth into singing and cry aloud, you who did not travail with child! For the [spiritual] children of the desolate one will be more than the children of the married wife, says the Lord. Enlarge the place of your tent, and let the curtains of your habitations be stretched out; spare not; lengthen your cords and strengthen your stakes. For you will spread abroad to the right hand and to the left; and your offspring will possess the nations and make the desolate cities to be inhabited. Fear not, for you shall not be ashamed; neither be confounded and depressed, for you shall not be put to shame. For you shall forget the shame of your youth, and you shall not [seriously] remember the reproach of your widowhood any more (Isaiah 54:1-4)

You afflicted [city], storm-tossed and not comforted, behold, I will set your stones in fair colours [in antimony to enhance their brilliance] and lay your foundations with sapphires. And I will make your windows and pinnacles of [sparkling] agates or rubies, and your gates of [shining] carbuncles, and all your walls [of your enclosures] of precious stones (Isaiah 54:11-12)

But He replied to them, Give them something to eat yourselves. And they said to Him, Shall we go and buy 200 denarii [about forty dollars] worth of bread and give it to them to eat? And He said to them, how many loaves do you have? Go and see. And when they [had looked and] knew, they said, Five [loaves] and two fish (Mark 6:37-38)

Then He commanded the people all to recline on the green grass by companies (Mark 6:39)

And taking the five loaves and two fish, He looked up to heaven and, praising God, gave thanks and broke the loaves and kept on giving them to the disciples to set before the people; and He [also] divided the two fish among [them] all (Mark 6:41)

And they all ate and were satisfied (Mark 6:42)

And He went up into the boat with them, and the wind ceased (sank to rest as if exhausted by its own beating). And they were astonished exceedingly [beyond measure] (Mark 6:51)

...................and as many as touched Him were restored to health (Mark 6: 56)

And He said to her, Because of this saying, you may go your way; the demon has gone out of your daughter [permanently]. And she went home and found the child thrown on the couch, and the demon departed (Mark 7: 29-30)

And they were overwhelmingly astonished, saying, He has done everything excellently (commendably and nobly)! He even makes the deaf to hear and the dumb to speak! (Mark 7:37)

Breaking the power of the spirit of idleness.....whoever desires to be great among you must be your servant. And whoever wishes to be most important and first in rank among you must be slave of all (Mark 10:43-44)

And her neighbours and relatives heard that the Lord had shown great mercy on her, and they rejoiced with her (Luke 1:58)

Blessed (praised and extolled and thanked) be the Lord, the God of Israel, because He has come and brought deliverance and redemption to His people! And He has raised up a Horn of salvation [a mighty and valiant Helper, the Author of salvation] for us in the house of David His servant— This is as He promised by the mouth of His holy prophets from the most ancient times [in the memory of man] — That we should have deliverance and be saved from our enemies and from the hand of all who detest and pursue us with hatred. To make true and show the mercy and compassion and kindness [promised] to our forefathers and to remember and carry out His holy covenant [to bless, which is all the more sacred because it is made by God Himself]. That covenant He sealed by oath to our forefather Abraham: To grant us that we, being delivered from the hand of our foes, might serve Him fearlessly. (Luke 1: 68-74)

And as He was praying, the appearance of His countenance became altered (different), and His raiment became dazzling white [flashing with the brilliance of lightning]. And behold, two men were conversing with Him—Moses and Elijah, Who appeared in splendour and majesty and brightness ……….. (Luke 9: 29-31)

However I tell you truly, there are some of those standing here who will not taste death before they see the kingdom of God. Now about eight days after these teachings, Jesus took with Him Peter and John and James and went up on the mountain to pray. And as He was praying, the appearance of His countenance became altered (different), and His raiment became dazzling white [flashing with the brilliance of lightning]. And behold, two men were conversing with Him—Moses and Elijah, Who appeared in splendour and majesty and brightness and were speaking of His exit [from life], which He was about to bring to realization at Jerusalem. Now Peter and those with him were weighed down with sleep, but when they fully awoke, they saw His glory (splendour and majesty and brightness) and the two men who stood with Him (Luke 9: 27-32)

And they have overcome (conquered) him by means of the blood of the Lamb and by the utterance of their testimony.... (Revelation 12:11)

Scriptures on Longevity

Then the Lord said, My Spirit shall not forever dwell and strive with man, for he also is flesh; but his days shall yet be 120 years (Genesis 6:3)

Behold, I establish My covenant or pledge with you and with your descendants after you (Genesis 9:9)

I will establish My covenant or pledge with you: Never again shall all flesh be cut off by the waters of a flood; neither shall there ever again be a flood to destroy the earth and make it corrupt (Genesis 9:11)

I will [earnestly] remember My covenant or solemn pledge which is between Me and you and every living creature of all flesh; and the waters will no more become a flood to destroy and make all flesh corrupt (Genesis 9:15)

The days of Abraham's life were 175 years. Then Abraham's spirit was released, and he died at a good (ample, full) old age, an old man, satisfied and satiated, and was gathered to his people (Genesis 25: 7-8)

......the days of Isaac were 180 years. And Isaac's spirit departed; he died and was gathered to his people, being an old man, satisfied and satiated with days; his sons Esau and Jacob buried him (Genesis 35:28-29)

Saying, If you will diligently hearken to the voice of the Lord your God and will do what is right in His sight, and will listen to and obey His commandments and keep all His statutes, I will put none of the diseases upon you which I brought upon the Egyptians, for I am the Lord Who heals you (Exodus 15:26)

Moses was 120 years old when he died; his eye was not dim nor his natural force abated (Deuteronomy 34:7)

He was despised and rejected and forsaken by men, a Man of sorrows and pains, and acquainted with grief and sickness; and like one from whom men hide their faces He was despised, and we did not appreciate His worth or have any esteem for Him. Surely He has borne our grief's (sicknesses, weaknesses, and distresses) and carried our sorrows and pains [of punishment], yet we [ignorantly] considered Him stricken, smitten, and afflicted by God [as if with leprosy]. But He was wounded for our transgressions, He was bruised for our guilt and iniquities; the chastisement [needful to obtain] peace and well-being for us was upon Him, and with the stripes [that wounded] Him we are healed and made whole. All we like sheep have gone astray, we have turned everyone to his own way; and the Lord has made to light upon Him the guilt and iniquity of us all (Isaiah 53: 3-6)

Forsake not [Wisdom], and she will keep, defend, and protect you; love her, and she will guard you (Proverbs 4:6)

Thus says the Lord: As the juice [of the grape] is found in the cluster, and one says, Do not destroy it, for there is a blessing in it, so will I do for My servants' sake, that I may not destroy them all (Isaiah 65:8)

But be glad and rejoice forever in that which I create; for behold, I create Jerusalem to be a rejoicing and her people a joy. And I will rejoice in Jerusalem and be glad in My people; and the sound of weeping will no more be heard in it, nor the cry of distress. There shall no more be in it an infant who lives but a few days, or an old man who dies prematurely; for the child shall die a hundred years old, and the sinner who dies when only a hundred years old shall be [thought only a child, cut off because he is] accursed. They shall build houses and inhabit them, and they shall plant vineyards and eat the fruit of them (Isaiah 65: 18-21)

When Jesus received the message, He said, This sickness is not to end in death; but [on the contrary] it is to honour God and to promote His glory, that the Son of God may be glorified through (by) it (John 11:4)

For these things took place, that the Scripture might be fulfilled (verified, carried out), Not one of His bones shall be broken (John 19: 36)

Whatever Is Worth Doing Must Be Done Well

Without allowing anything to hold you back, do what you are doing well to the glory of The Lord.

About The Book

The Bible tells us that the last enemy that shall be subdued and abolished is death (1 Corinthians 15:26). This book has been written to bring into the light the truth that, for everyone in Christ, death has no authority over us. Christian Faith is a covenant of longevity. Satan and its agents has no authority over the truly born again Children of The Almighty God. We must not at any point enter into agreement with death or satan about anything to advance its kingdom, especially after we have confessed Jesus Christ as our Lord and Saviour. We must not enter into covenant with satan concerning anything, satan cannot satisfy us, satan hasn't got what we needs, satan cannot supply our needs, satan hasn't got what it takes for anyone to be alive in this world. Only God through Jesus Christ can satisfy us and meets our needs.

BOOKS AUTHORED BY FOLAKE HASSAN

God is Good

We All Have Reasons to Praise God

The Names of God

The Attributes of God

Coming Out of Bondage

Be Encouraged

No Death in Jesus Christ

BECOMING A CHRISTIAN

Becoming a Christian is not a difficult task at all. The Holy Bible instructs every mankind to be born again by confessing our sin and accept Jesus Christ as our Lord and Saviour by praying a simple prayer of salvation.

The Prayer of Salvation

Father God, I come to You in the Name of Jesus Christ. According to your Word in the book of Roman 10:9, which says "If you acknowledge and confess with your lips that Jesus is Lord and in your heart believe (adhere to, trusts in, and rely on the truth) that God raised Him from the dead, you will be saved.

I confess Jesus Christ as my Lord and Saviour, Lord Jesus come into my life and forgive me for all my sins. Be Lord of my life in Jesus name, Amen.

Congratulations if you have just prayed this prayer, you are now a Christian and you are saved.

You now have rights to all the promises of God in the Holy Bible.

I will advise you to read the Holy Bible and other Christian literatures regularly to build up your faith in the Lord. Also you will need a Word based church to attend regularly. Be part of a good local church that teaches Christian to grow in The Word of God.

*****Please write to us to inform us of your new decision you made to become a Christian and we will continue to offer all helps necessary for you to grow in Christ.

Remain Blessed

Yours in Christ

Folake Hassan (Mrs)

Founder/President: The Blessed Christian Centre

ABOUT THE AUTHOR

Folake Hassan is the Author of the books titled "The Attributes of God", "Coming Out of Bondage" "Be Encouraged" and several other books. She is the Owner of The Online Christian Bookshop named The Blessed Christian: www.theblessedchristian.co.uk . It is Folake's passion to see souls saved and confess Jesus Christ as their Lord and Saviour. Folake Hassan is blessed with 3 children with the youngest being 19 years of age at the time of writing this book. Folake and her children lives in London, United Kingdom.

www.ingramcontent.com/pod-product-compliance
Lightning Source LLC
Chambersburg PA
CBHW052011090426

42741CB00008B/1644